Leap Days

Leap Days

Chronicles of a Midlife Move

Katherine Lanpher

SPRINGBOARD PRESS

NEW YORK BOSTON

Springboard Press
Hachette Book Group USA
1271 Avenue of the Americas, New York, NY 10020
Visit our Web site at www.HachetteBookGroupUSA.com

Springboard Press is an imprint of Warner Books, Inc. The Springboard name and logo are trademarks of Hachette Book Group USA.

First Edition: October 2006

The author gratefully acknowledges permission to reprint "A Blessing" by James Wright from *The Branch Will Not Break* (Wesleyan University Press, 1963), © 1963 by James Wright. Reprinted with the permission of Wesleyan University Press.

The author also acknowledges with gratitude that portions of this book include material previously published on the op-ed pages of the *New York Times:* "A Manhattan Admonition," August 31, 2004, and "A Long Wait for Winter," February 11, 2003. Portions of this book are also adapted from material previously published in *More* magazine: "'The Magic of Machu Picchu," *More*, December 2005 / January 2006, and "A Tale of Two Cities," *More*, June 2005.

Library of Congress Cataloging-in-Publication Data

Lanpher, Katherine.
    Leap days : chronicles of a midlife move / Katherine Lanpher. — 1st ed.
        p.   cm.
    ISBN-10: 0-8212-5830-3
    ISBN-13: 978-0-8212-5830-9
    1. Lanpher, Katherine.   2. Television personalities — United States — Biography.   3. Radio broadcasters — United States — Biography.
I. Title.

PN1992.4.L32A3 2006
791.4502'8092 — dc22   2006010491

10   9   8   7   6   5   4   3   2   1

For my parents,
Donald and Jean Lanpher

Contents

Leap Days

Flying Lessons

I AM STANDING on a platform two stories above the terra firma of Manhattan. In my right hand, I hold the bar of a trapeze swing. The swing pulls me forward, and the only thing keeping me on the platform is the sure hold my trapeze instructor has on the loop of my safety harness. This is not the time to think about my trust issues. My left hand is frozen in its grip to a metal stand on the platform.

I'm supposed to let go.

But I can't.

If I look straight ahead, I can see the towers of Battery Park City, close to Ground Zero. If I look right, I can see the blue-gray waters of the Hudson. I don't look left because I'm too busy looking down. That's where the safety net is.

Manny, the instructor, starts to talk to me gently, the way you would talk to someone perched on a building ledge. Only in this case you want the person to jump.

"I've got you," he says. "I've held on to men who weigh more than three times what you do. I've got you, so you can take your left hand and put it on the bar."

My toes are curled over the edge of the platform, just as Manny told me. I am trying to jut my hips out, just the way Manny told me. But when I lift my left hand from its perch of seeming safety, I don't feel Manny's hold on me; I feel the trapeze bar pulling me down, down, down, to trapeze fatality and, even worse — embarrassment. I return to my death clutch on the iron railing.

You might ask how I got here.

I could tell you it's because for more than a year now I have cycled past the nets and swings of this trapeze school set up by the river, and I have always stopped, caught by the spectacle of someone volunteering for flight.

Or I could tell you that it feels as though I've already made bigger jumps.

Manny is pushing me a little now, to show me he really is back there to make sure I won't fall. It's not often you get a safety harness in life, and I decide to trust this one. My left hand goes to the trapeze bar, and to my surprise, I'm right where I should be. I'm wobbling a little, but I'm still there, balanced on the edge of the platform.

"OK," Manny says. "When I say, 'Hup!' you'll jump."

The cry rings through the air: "One-two-three-HUP!"

I spring up on my feet and jump — right back onto the platform. I have gone exactly nowhere.

"No, Katherine." I hear the bemused voice of Manny behind me. "You have to jump *forward*.

"HUP!"

The same thing happens. Several times. It turns out that I am great at jumping in place. And then — I don't know if Manny pushes me or if I spring forward of my own will — I am whooshing through the air, hanging from the trapeze, my body arcing as I swing forward and then back and forward and then back.

I'm flying.

On Leap Day 2004 I took an actual leap, leaving behind the Midwestern city where I came of age, married, divorced, worked, lived, loved, and prospered for more than two decades, to move to New York. I cried so hard at the airport curb that the strangers milling around me must have thought I was on my way to a funeral. If they had offered me condolences, I would have accepted them. I felt, in fact, that a loved one was dying, that a life so known and dear to me was ending: my old, soon-to-be-former, settled life, in which I knew the tracks of the coming days the way I knew without looking where the spoons were in my silverware drawer. Someone was pushing that woman off the platform, and it was me. There was no safety net. Before that day, I had been an earthbound creature: think root vegetable. Now I was on my way to a new job, a new life, and a new city where I could count the number of friends I had on one hand. I was a few months shy of my forty-fifth birthday, a confirmed daughter of the prairie who had grown up in Moline, Illinois, gone to college and graduate school in Chicago, and then moved to St. Paul, Minnesota. I was as Midwestern as weak coffee at supper and ham sandwiches at a funeral lunch. I never did understand why Chicago was called the Second City when it was always the First City to me. The water and the valleys of the Hudson were unknown to me; I was bound for life to the muddy currents of the Mississippi.

So why was I getting on a plane to New York? Well, as I like to tell people, on Leap Day 2004 I moved to midlife and had a Manhattan crisis.

I had never meant to live in New York. Then again, I had never meant to become a middle-aged woman with bifocals either. It's funny how that happens. One day, your thirties seem to stretch in front of you for what feels like a luxurious length of time, and the next you don't quite recognize that woman in the mirror. I have friends who say soothingly, "Oh, you're not middle-aged," and all I can think is that just because I'm older doesn't mean I have lost my ability to do arithmetic. The odds that I will live to be a hundred are slim. You do the math; I'm middle-aged.

I don't think I moved to Manhattan because I was having a midlife crisis, but I know it looks that way. Some women get their hair dyed; this woman gave up a life and community she'd invested twenty years in to start over in a metropolis that is a fulcrum of youth and power. Midway through the journey of his life, Dante found himself in a dark wood; midway through my life, I found myself in New York and my own version of a divine comedy. I came of age in the Midwest; I came of middle age in Manhattan.

So I'm flying through the air next to the Hudson River. Pedestrians who stopped to witness my fear on the platform now stop to applaud my flight. Django, one of the other instructors, is manipulating the rigging to my safety harness as I fly.

"Hey, Katherine!" he yells up to me. "You can say something, you know."

I can hear him laughing. Well, at least I'm amusing him. Earlier, all of the instructors had shown the sort of diffidence you expect from the wranglers at a dude ranch when they're forced to haul out Brownie, the thirteen-year-old pony, for the tourist who can't ride.

I manage one word and it's this: "Down."

On his count, I let go of the bar and flop into the safety net. I bounce my way to the dismount area, and it's here that I encounter my real fear. To get back on the ground, I am supposed to somersault onto a padded mat some six feet below me.

Now this, I think, is crazy. I would rather leap off a pedestal into thin air — I would rather do it twice — than be forced to somersault into a six-foot drop.

"I can't do it," I hear myself say.

Django grins. He's amiable — tall, lean, and rangy, probably in his early twenties, with a head of auburn dreadlocks.

"C'mon," he says. "You were just on the trapeze. You can do this."

No, I tell him, I can't.

Here's what I don't tell him: When I signed up for this class, I had anticipated my fear of heights. I had anticipated my fear of flying. I had anticipated my control issues. What I hadn't counted on was my childhood nemesis: tumbling. I have floundered at it since grade school, and all the weekends at the Turners Club with little gymnasts in pink leotards never helped me. I feared it then and I still hate it now. In junior high, I once took a D rather than try to do a backward somersault in gym class. I still remember Miss Baum pleading with me, "You'll lose your place on the honor roll!" Normally, this was an argument that would have convinced me to perform any number of untold stunts, but in this case, I didn't care. I hated it that much.

I begin to panic; I can't move. I really, really can't do this. Tears spring into my eyes. Django looks annoyed. The next student can't fly until my can has left the safety net, and my can apparently isn't moving. "Just put your hands here," he says, indicating two loops woven into the side of the net, "and then flip over and I'll catch you."

"I think I have trust issues," I spit out. Now I feel like I'm going to hyperventilate. "Can't I just sort of roll over or jump?"

Django shakes his head. Nope. I could really hurt myself that way.

"Can't I just . . . ?"

Django loses patience. "If you want," he snaps, "you can crawl over to the ladder and climb down."

I look and then realize that getting onto the ladder will require me to swing my body several feet through the air so that my hands can reach and grab on to the rungs — and this is without a safety harness. It's death either way, that's for sure, and I choose the path where at least someone is going to spot me. I clutch the cloth loops, shimmy half my body over the net, tuck my head, and roll.

Django flips me over and I stand upright, a slightly shaken, slightly overweight woman who hates to tumble but loves to fly.

I want to go back up.

You might ask what midlife has to do with Manhattan.

The answer is change. Walk the same block in this city for even a few months and you witness transformation — the tiny flower shop morphs into a designer perfumery, the video store suddenly pops up as an espresso joint. Scaffolding and plywood can appear overnight on any given corner, and you can track the daily evolutions on your way to the subway.

Change is such a constant here that people have to become accustomed to it, if not inured. Novelist Colson Whitehead was thinking of the transitory nature of the storefronts and corners when he wrote that you become a New Yorker "when what was there before is more solid and real than what is here now." That fine newspaperman of the old school, Pete Hamill, calls New York the Capital of Nostalgia. In his book *Downtown: My Manhattan,* he tells us that the New York version of nostalgia isn't just about buildings and the people who live in them: "It involves an almost fatalistic acceptance of the permanent presence of loss. Nothing will ever stay the same. Tuesday turns into Wednesday and something valuable is behind you forever. An 'is' has become a 'was.'"

I read those words the first summer I was here, registering an empathetic pang. I had left a job as the host of a regional public radio show to come to New York for a shot at a national audience, as cohost for Al Franken as he jump-started the liberal Air America Radio network. It was a calculated risk. Before that point, I had lived a life that followed a careful path; I was vested with a pension when I was twenty-seven. Now I was working as a sidekick for a start-up operation so high profile that I could read in the *Wall Street Journal* about why we didn't make payroll. The week I discovered the payments on our health-care policies had lapsed, I panicked and called my former boss in St. Paul and asked if my old job was still open. He called me back to announce in sorrowful tones that the operative sentiment was that if I wanted to go away so bad, I could stay away. I felt like an "is" who had become a "was." And while my loss wasn't quite the same, I was feeling an overwhelming longing for my old life, its sweetness and its security. I started to joke with friends that I had become an urban version of a hobbit: all I really wanted to do was go back to the Shire. In New York, my life appeared to me in stark outline. I was divorced, childless, and alone in a new city. There were days I walked the streets and thought, *How did I get here?*

To accept that you are middle-aged means to accept a permanent presence of loss, that Tuesdays are overtaken by Wednesdays, that your thirties have been trumped by your forties — and that they'll soon be trumped by your fifties and sixties and so on. I had already felt loss in my life, and it felt like a harsh bargain that now I had to accept it as a constant presence. I missed those days when I was younger, when thinking about the future gave me the rich feeling of infinite chances, that my future was hemmed in only by the choices I made. It's hard to let that feeling go, to square your shoulders and look at finite reality, to accept that maybe there are going to be only one or two more chances at transformation left.

And that's why, when the offer came to move to New York, I took it.

I wasn't sure how many more chances would come my way.

Of the crew assembled this afternoon for our trapeze lesson, a woman named Paulette is closest to me in age and spirit. Her brother had bought her a gift certificate to the aerialist school for her fiftieth birthday. Our other classmates include a tattooed graphic artist who is on his fourth week of lessons, a slender woman with a slight British accent, and a boyfriend/ girlfriend duo from Brooklyn in their early twenties.

Manny gives us his opening spiel about how we'll learn to hang from our knees on the trapeze, and how we'll learn to do a backflip off the swing. When I ask, "Um, is it OK if we just swing? Because that was the height of my ambitions," it is Paulette who laughs and nods in empathy.

When Paulette gets to the top of the platform, she balks.

"I just can't do this," I hear her say. "I'm sorry. I can't."

On the ground, Django mutters, "Hope she does it. Hope she doesn't come down."

Paulette starts to climb off the platform.

"C'mon, do it," Django says under his breath. He turns to me and adds, "Ninety percent of the people who climb down the first time, they don't go back up."

When Paulette gets her feet back on the ground, I want to put my arm around her.

"It's that left bar, isn't it?" I say. "I know exactly how you feel."

"It's scarier than I thought," she says. "A lot scarier."

When it's Paulette's turn again, she hesitates, but we all urge her to go back up. When she ascends the ladder the second time, I am fairly sure she'll succeed. But she pauses on the platform for what seems like many minutes, and I realize that inside my head I am repeating a trapeze mantra for her: *You can do it, you can do it, you can do it.* Finally, she gives a hesitant jump and swings through the air. Our whole class cheers.

I'm reminded of how, as a child, I was terrified by the deep end of the pool. I would wade from the shallows to the dip in the pool floor that indicated deeper water, but once I had to tread water to stay afloat, once my feet hit that watery nothingness instead of the tile at the bottom of the pool, my fear would always draw me back. When I finally started going into the deep end, I would crouch by the edge of the pool and then fall into the water like a dropped piece of fruit, scuttling back to the side as soon as I surfaced. It took a long time before I could just dive in with aplomb.

And that's the thing about trapeze. You can't sidle into it. And for most of my life, I've been a really good sidler.

Django says to me later, "You came here by yourself, didn't you? Looks like you made some friends."

"Well, sure," I tell him. "Bomb threats, subway fires, trapeze lessons — they're all bonding experiences."

"Those are good analogies for trapeze," he says, smirking.

Not really, I want to say. Trapeze is a good analogy for life.

The reason I climb back up the ladder to the platform isn't because of the sense of flight. What I like is the moment before I reach for the swing, the moment of anticipation before my left hand grabs on to the bar and I am trembling on the edge and it is up to me and the count of one-two-three-HUP!

It turns out I like to leap.

What Iowa Did to Manhattan

Not that long ago, I was in the apartment of some friends of mine and they introduced me to their neighbor, a banker who works downtown and lives in the Village, a woman who grew up in New Jersey. She and I exchanged pleasantries, and then, giving me a friendly, appraising look, she asked where I was from.

I hate that. I was pretty sure I knew what was coming next. I smiled and told her that I had moved to New York after living in Minnesota for many years. She nodded. "That explains the twang."

Excuse me?

"You have a twang," she said confidently. "You've got that Midwestern twang."

Oh, the things I could have said in response, such as, "No,

that's not a twang, that's what English sounds like." Instead, I mumbled a terse reply and stepped into the kitchen, where I promptly gave myself a twang-free talking-to: *Why am I getting so uptight? Who cares if I sound like I come from Illinois or Minnesota? After all, I do come from there.* So I returned to the living room, determined to be less defensive about my Midwestern roots. I apologized, made a few jokes about my prairie-based speech patterns, and was just congratulating myself on how I had navigated this set of social rapids when the banker leaned forward with another question.

"You use the word 'crik,' right?" she asked.

"Only when I'm down in the holler" came out of my mouth before I could stop myself.

I was just about to apologize again when I realized that she thought I was serious. And that's when it hit me: she thought I was Tammy.

You remember Tammy, played first by Debbie Reynolds and then by Sandra Dee, the corn-fed character from Mississippi whose full name was Tammy Tyree? Who brought along a goat when she attended college? Whose adventures were detailed in such films as *Tammy and the Bachelor* and *Tammy Tell Me True?*

I a-reckon many of you do.

I was going to explain the geographic distance between, say, Mississippi and Minnesota, and then I just shut up. For some New Yorkers, there is no difference between the South and Garrison Keillor country, between people from Mississippi, Minnesota, or, for that matter, Montana. After all, those people are all from the same place: not New York. You can talk about provincialism all you want, but all you will get from them is pity. After all, they grew up in the greatest city on Earth or, more likely, in its shadow. And you didn't. When these New Yorkers are searching for a word to describe some poor rube, they will pull out the closest approximation that comes to mind and then to mouth: "Midwesterner" or "Kansan" or — the ne plus ultra of a New Yorker put-down — "Iowan."

I once asked a woman who lived in Tribeca what Iowa had ever done to Manhattan. She gave me a dimpled smile and said sweetly, "Everything."

She was from Michigan.

So that night, in my guise of Tammy, I tethered the goat and brushed the hayseed from my shoulders, determined that I would enjoy the rest of the evening.

Lord willin' and the crik don't rise.

Language shapes us. And it was true that during my first few months in New York, people didn't understand me. There clearly was a city patois that I hadn't picked up, a set of phrases and customs that I kept bumping into the way a sparrow will fly into a glass window over and over again.

I'm at the bodega — that's the corner grocery — across the street from my apartment building. It is a dimly lit, small shop, crammed from floor to ceiling with everything from Pepperidge Farm cookies to condoms, from Kitty Litter to four flavors of Mexican soda. There is a tiny grill and a steam table for the breakfast and lunch trade that keeps the place full-to-bursting from morning to midafternoon with construction workers, deliverymen, and neighborhood residents. I'm here to order breakfast.

"An egg and cheese on a bun, please."

The guy behind the grill counter just looks at me.

"Toasted," I say for good measure. "Could you toast the bun?"

He's still looking at me. I am trying to figure out what I did wrong. This is a classic New York breakfast, up there with the corn muffin when it comes to indigenous Manhattan morning foods.

I point to the display case of bread. Comprehension dawns across his face. It's a roll, he tells me with great care, and then he enunciates the word and stretches it out for me so that I, poor witless creature, will understand. Rolllll, not bun. Rolllllll. Here, say it with me.

Roll. Got it.

I move down the line and stand in front of the cash register. My egg and cheese appears, wrapped in white paper, and the clerk behind the cash register tries to put it in a plastic bag.

"That's OK," I say, "I don't need the sack."

The what?

I sigh. Bag, sack, whatever. I am still learning how to hail a taxi, how to give directions to a cabbie, how to decipher the subway system. I was hoping that I could at least order breakfast. I was wrong.

★　　★　　★

All I want is a space for my bike.

When I had looked at the apartment that became my home, I had been told there was a bike room in the building.

"Humph," says the morning doorman. "I don't know about that. You'll have to talk to Gus."

"A what? You want a what?" says another building employee. "I'll have to ask. Try Gus."

Gus is the building superintendent. I finally track him down.

"Ahhhh," he says with sad eyes. "There's one in the basement."

I brighten. This is good news.

"It's full," he adds.

A few days later, I am talking to a veteran New Yorker who has called to see how I am adjusting to the city.

"Have you given the baksheesh yet?" she asks.

The what?

"The baksheesh."

I pause. I am afraid it is more Yiddish, more evidence of my ignorance. I arrived with what I thought were a few key words of Yiddish, such as "shiksa" (a derogatory term for a non-Jewish female) and "meshuggeneh" (crazy). They are not enough. I am learning a new Yiddish word about every other day.

As it turns out, however, "baksheesh" is Persian.

"Here's what you do," she says. "You get a nice card for

your super and you write that you are looking forward to starting your new life in New York with the building and the people who work there. Then you put in a hundred dollars. Does he have anyone working for him?"

Two people.

"Then you do the same for them, only put in a little less. Let me tell you, I don't call for anything in my building unless they can see that I'm standing at the door with something green in my hand."

This puzzles me. After all, isn't it in their job descriptions to help people? You would think I had moved to some distant Eastern European country before the fall of the Iron Curtain, someplace where the entire economy depends on small bills being passed from hand to hand on the black market or where people trade goods for services. I imagine myself with a babushka tied under my chin, pleading with Gus in a darkened stairwell and proffering a swinging piece of poultry: "Here, good chicken for bike rack."

I think that if I had tried to tip anyone doing his or her job back home in Minnesota, it would have been taken as an insult. Here, it is an insult not to give a tip. And I realize: I am in a foreign country. I had better start acting like it. Where is that babushka?

I follow the baksheesh instructions. Two days later, someone, somehow, miraculously finds a space in the bike room for me. Thus emboldened, I begin to tip everyone, everywhere. When a friend from Minnesota comes to help me out with my move, staying at my apartment during the day to accept the various deliveries of goods and services, I give her a knowing lecture on the tips I have set aside for each expected person. She looks at me kind of funny, but I assure her — with all the annoying authority that someone who has lived in the city for two weeks can muster — that this is just how it is done.

So you can imagine my surprise a month or so later when I tell this story to a colleague, who looks at me, laughs, and says, "You tipped the cable guy? The Cable Guy?"

That, it turns out, is meshuggeneh.

Who knew?

There is a right way and a wrong way to hail a cab.

If you are headed downtown, then you should not get in a cab headed uptown. You might think to yourself, *Who cares? All the driver has to do is turn a corner and he's headed downtown.* You would be wrong in that assertion. If you want to go downtown but find you are on a one-way street headed uptown, then you best walk a few blocks over to a street where the traffic is headed in the right direction. If you don't, then you have broken an unwritten rule of life here and you will be treated accordingly.

Trust me on this one. Glares issue from the occupant of the driver's seat and, occasionally, so do wagging fingers and diatribes of abuse. It does not matter that you carry with you in your head a film clip of transportation in New York. In this brief mise-en-scène, you raise a hand, a yellow cab glides to a halt, you give an address, and you are off. But that is not how it works in reality, and you discover this the day you are chastised in Urdu. Well, you are pretty sure it was Urdu. It doesn't really matter what the language was: the message was successfully transmitted.

Kindly New Yorkers who want to save you from trouble also try to explain this to you. Here is what you don't say to them: it ALL looks like downtown to you. You carry with you a color-coded laminated map so that you can tell when you cross from Midtown into Murray Hill or slide from the East Village into Nolita. You are at dinner with a native New Yorker and you bring the map out onto the restaurant table. "Put it away," she says under her breath, as if I have just put a dog turd on the table. She doesn't want anyone to think we are tourists. She is too late.

I am, essentially, a tourist with a lot of luggage, planning on a long-term stay. I hum the song from *On the Town* as a sort of musical map: "New York, New York, it's a wonderful town, / The Bronx is up, the Battery's down." Betty Comden and Adolph Green are known for their lyrics; I'm just grateful for their sense of direction.

You are coming back with a new acquaintance from a reading by Toni Morrison in Central Park. You take the subway home, the No. 1. Your new friend scans the subway stop and then stands at a particular spot. You ask him why. He explains that if he stands there, then he'll get into a car perfectly chosen so that when the subway pulls into our Christopher Street stop, the doors will open directly in front of the exit and its turnstiles. No crowd, no shuffling through lines of people, we'll sail right through.

The first time I do this by myself, my delight knows no bounds.

And I think, *Maybe I can live here.*

I first encountered New York when I was a college freshman in Chicago, and a new girl moved into the dorm room next door. Her name was Lissa and she was the daughter of a famous fiction editor — I, of course, had never heard of him — and she had her own shrink on Central Park West. Her boyfriend was a jazz musician at the Berklee College of Music in Boston, and she couldn't wait to transfer out of this dump and go to Yale, where she belonged.

I, on the other hand, hailed from Moline, Illinois. I was still proud of my thespian swan song as one of the leads in the Moline Senior High production of *Arsenic and Old Lace*. I didn't know anyone my age who had her own psychiatrist and, even better, boasted about his address. I thought my White Stag–brand parka, so new it creaked, was the latest in fashion. I was still secretly sorry I had never made the dance line team.

We fascinated each other. She would walk around me in circles in my dorm room and ask me questions, practically clapping her hands in delight at my answers. For her, I was an honest-to-goodness anthropological find: "The Girl from the Midwest." My life story literally made her laugh.

I did nothing to dispel her delight. She wanted to know about hayrack rides? Fine, I would tell her about hayrack rides. If some part of me knew that she was treating me like a Kewpie doll, the other part of me didn't want to acknowledge it. I enjoyed the attention and I liked hearing her stories of this other world, all tall buildings and bright lights and famous people. I imagined her walking across Central Park to her psychiatrist's office, I imagined her, underage, in smoky jazz bars and attending Broadway shows and walking through streets choked with traffic. In short, I imagined her in every picture I had ever seen of Manhattan, whether it fit her actual life or not. She was my anthropological find: "The Girl from New York."

She had known a modicum of fame on her father's side and struggle on her mother's side after her father left the family. She was very, very bright — the kind of person for whom Hannah Arendt was light and familiar reading — and she was very, very alienating. Nothing in Chicago was good enough for her — the food, the transit, the people — they all paled in comparison to what she had known in New York. Everyone and everything was a target for her critical mind and sharp tongue. Professors adored her, but she was less than popular among my circle of friends. I called an old roommate and asked if she remembered Lissa. Her reply was blunt: "She was pure evil."

We were all cramming for a final exam one night when Lissa announced there was no way she was going to take that test until she had more time to study. She would get an extension. How? By slamming a nail into her forehead and claiming injury. She showed up the next day with a ragged bandanna wrapped around her forehead and an extension. Did she really do it? I don't know. She had a gift for persuasion.

Lissa thought she was ugly, or someone had persuaded her she was ugly, but I thought she had an interesting face, with sharp green eyes, a pointed chin, and thin lips that curved easily into a smile or pulled into a grimace. Years later, when I read about how her father could send students reeling from his writing seminars, lacerated by his outbursts, I thought of Lissa and how she could do the same and how the same must have been done to her.

I have carried a picture of her in my mind's eye for decades now:

I am standing outside our dormitory. Lissa is leaving, going back to the East Coast. She will not return; she has achieved her transfer to Yale. Someone — her boyfriend? I can't remember — is giving her a ride in a station wagon that is so stuffed she is crouched against the rear window. The car pulls away and Lissa looks back at us standing by the door, one of her hands on the back window for balance. She doesn't smile or wave, she just stares; for a moment she looks like a small animal, uncertain what will happen next.

I understood then that she might have been scared underneath all the bombast, that she might have been vulnerable underneath the scorn. Years afterward, whenever I thought about New York, I would think about all the names she dropped, the stories she told about Manhattan landmarks, and then I would remember that last image of her, frightened. She looked caged. She was a small reason — but still, a reason — why I didn't feel a strong urge to move to Manhattan when I was young. I didn't think I had the fortitude. I didn't want to pay the price.

But I do end up in New York. At the end of my first week, I am abashed to discover that I am homesick. The giddiness that came from the quickness of the move has dissipated and now I am alone, in an apartment that is still only half-assembled. The walls are bare. I sit and look at the boxes and watch a biting snow pelt my windows. If I were home in Minnesota, I could call a friend for dinner or walk across the street to talk to my neighbors. If I were home. I'm not home and that's the problem. I think of all the friends who told me I was so brave to make this move at my age. At this moment, I don't feel very brave; I feel very, very small.

Even the snow looks different here. I cast about for what to do and decide that a stylish fortysomething New York career woman might go and get her nails done. Now *that* is something I couldn't do back in St. Paul on a Sunday evening.

The brightly lit nail shop is bustling, and the Korean woman who greets me asks the usual battery of questions while she examines my hands. How long have I lived here? Oh, I'm new. Where did I move from? How do I like it here?

I answer all her queries, and then I lean over the narrow table to confess, "Actually, I'm pretty homesick."

Her eyes narrow, she sucks in some breath, and then she barks out an uppercase admonition: "DON'T BE BIG BABY."

The women on either side of us turn to look. My interlocutor smiles.

"Now, give me your hands, beautiful," she says. "Oval or square?"

I laugh so hard I nearly fall off my chair.

And then I try to take her advice.

I don't know how long it takes to make someone a New Yorker, but I have heard plenty of theories.

"The first six months are the worst," one friend counsels, regaling me with tales of how he used to sit on a bare mattress in his studio apartment, looking at the walls and thinking about all his friends back home who had houses and mortgages and beds that stood off the floor.

"You need at least a year," says a friend who lived on the Upper West Side for about that long, having accepted a fellowship at Columbia. She remembers the day when she found herself fighting over a cab during a driving rain and how she won the battle, turning to tell her opponent, "That's life in the big city."

Then there is the auburn-haired acting coach I meet at a book party. She shakes her long earrings and pronounces the incubation term for a New Yorker — "Three years. At least." — in much the same tones that I have heard judges discuss mandatory minimum sentencing.

There is a rainy day when I get on the subway and scoot over to an unaccountably empty seat, relieved that I have found one in this crowded car. As soon as I sit down, I realize why it was unoccupied: there is an indentation in the seat and it is full of water from someone's umbrella. I stand up, water sopping from my coat but my heart full of gratitude. "Thank God it wasn't urine," I tell myself.

For a while, I told that story to people, thinking it was proof that I was becoming a New Yorker. But then I saw the man with the ukulele.

It was just the other day, on West 10th Street. He had a timeworn face with some stubble and he wore an old wool cap with a brim and a dark overcoat. But what I noticed was the orange ukulele tucked under his arm, shining like a beacon against the coat. I was the only person to turn around and notice him. I know that because I followed him for a few blocks. No heads turned, no one pointed, no one asked, "Hey, why do you have an orange ukulele?" *Back home,* I thought, *if someone walked around with an orange ukulele, at least an eyebrow or two would go up.*

And I think that is why so many people want to live here, people with outsize dreams or big mouths or, say, a penchant for dressing in gender-inappropriate clothing. Because New York can accommodate you in a way that Iowa — or Minnesota, or Wisconsin — can't. You can walk down the street with an orange ukulele and no one will notice you, and that can be its own sort of blessing, its own communal inclusion. No one will notice you except for the woman trying to hail a cab going in the wrong direction, the woman with the goat.

Truth and Beauty in New York

I HAVE NEVER FELT SO UGLY as I did the first year I lived in New York. That may not surprise you, but it surprised me. Before my move, I liked to think of myself as a woman fairly secure in her own skin, a woman who had made peace with her body and her face. I had outlived a lot of beauty baggage — hot pants, Dorothy Hamill's pixie haircut, and liquid-protein diets come to mind, and that was all before I could vote. I had weathered enough cultural expectations about my appearance to achieve a kind of separate peace, especially if they were Eileen Fisher separates.

I have lived in Manhattan for only a few months when I wander into a little boutique just a few blocks from my apartment building, a storefront where the clothes are so clever they practically flirt with you through the glass. There is a jacket that mixes quilted leather with silk and tweed, a suit that manages to combine floral and plaids in a way that makes you look smarter for wearing it. The combinations of fabrics and textures are so inviting that I decide to investigate. I walk in, and as I start to browse, I find myself flipping faster and faster through the clothes. Here is a rack of blouses and here are their sizes: 0, 2, 2, 4. Over here are the pants: another 0, more 2s, a 4. I cross the shop and look at some dresses on hangers and find a size 10; this must be the Husky Girl section of the store. I walk over to a small desk, where the lone saleswoman — who had issued a bored hello when I opened the door — is reading a magazine.

"Excuse me," I say, "do you have any more tens? Or maybe a twelve in the back?"

She looks up, and her eyes brush quickly over my figure.

"I'm sorry," she says blandly, then shrugs, shaking her glossy black hair. "We don't really cut past an eight." Then she gives me a pinched size-2 smile and reverts to the glossy pages in her hand.

I want to smack her.

I want to lean over the desk, grip the magazine she is reading, and explain to her that in the free world, people trade legal tender for goods and that, to facilitate this trade, merchants often scale their goods to fit their customers. I want to tell her that the average American woman is five foot four and weighs 140 pounds and wears a size-14 dress. I want her to note that an eyeball estimate of the pedestrians passing in front of her shop would reveal that many such average women live RIGHT HERE in New York. I want to tell her she could PRINT money if she took two of those size-6 dresses and combined them into one. I want to strike a blow on behalf of all the women who will follow me into this store and receive the same snub. I want to take a knife, shave the offending flesh off my hips and belly, and leave the congealing bloody fat all over the floor.

"There," I want to say, "I think I've cut past an eight."

Instead, I stand there for a moment, a little stunned. Before I walked in, I was worried I wouldn't be able to afford the clothes; it didn't occur to me that even if I had the money, the clothes wouldn't want me. I quietly replace the dress on a rack and leave quickly, before the saleswoman has to call the fire department to use the Jaws of Life to get my fat ass through the door.

And I think to myself, *Welcome to New York.*

A few months later, I tell this story to another woman as we sit over drinks at the bar of the Gramercy Tavern. This woman is accomplished and elegant, with thick gray hair, bluntly cut and stylish. Mutual friends had arranged for us to meet, to soften my entry into life in Manhattan; more than a decade ago, she too had moved from the Midwest to New York. I tell her more than the story; I tell her I feel ugly. Is this normal for women in their forties who move here from somewhere else? Did anything like this happen when she first arrived in town?

She gives a physical start at the question, and I wince at

my own rudeness. I hadn't meant it the way it must have sounded. But then she gives me a searching look and, leaning forward, tells me about her first attempt to buy the sort of gown she would need for one of her new endeavors, when she would be attending many black-tie fund-raising events. And of how she went into a designer's shop and, after looking around, asked the salesman on the floor if he had any size 12s.

He drew himself up and exhaled noisily through his nose. "Perhaps," he said, "in the basement. I will have someone look."

We laugh. I realize later that we both were exchanging anecdotes about what one friend of mine calls "wallpaper moments," those awful instances of recognition when a woman realizes she doesn't quite register in the body public the way she used to, that she has in fact become relegated to the background like, well, wallpaper. We don't make your size, and if we do, it's in the basement. We'll have someone look.

When I was a young reporter in Minnesota, I was marooned for days in a small city with a group of other journalists, all of us covering a labor strike. After deadline one night, a group of us decamped to a bar where a prizewinning photographer was holding court. He was blond and bearded, with a weather-beaten face. He fancied himself a connoisseur of women and boasted that he could tell when a woman's beauty would peak; he proceeded to go through the women of his newsroom, explicating which one had reached the height of her looks and which one had yet to top out. Then, like one of those seers-for-hire who read tarot cards at a party, he extended the favor to those women sitting near him at the bar.

"You," he said, pointing to me, "you'll reach your peak in your early thirties."

I was twenty-six and just stupid enough to be glad that I hadn't "peaked" already.

In Melissa Bank's novel *The Wonder Spot*, protagonist Sophie Applebaum walks into a party at a Brooklyn loft and sees her junior counterparts: "The women are young, young, young, liquidy and sweet-looking; they are batter, and I am the sponge cake they don't know they'll become."

The women who walk past me on Bleecker, who collect in little cliques on Sixth Avenue, who bunch together on corners while shopping in Soho, are young, young, young, and so beautiful that sometimes it makes my heart ache. A young Indian woman nearly stopped me in my tracks one day near West 8th Street; I can recall with little effort her ruby-studded nose, her languid eyes, the way her low-slung jeans hung off the rosewood knobs of her hips. Or there was the ivory-skinned brunette who stood in a corner during a reading I attended on the Upper East Side, her cheeks flushed, her eyebrows dark marks of jet. She looked like a painting by John Singer Sargent. I tell myself I'm not nostalgic for my own youth when I see them, that I am nostalgic for their youth, that I know how they will feel a few decades from now, when life is less unthinking and more deliberate. And when I catch myself thinking like that, I wonder if I am any better, really, than the photographer who presumed that he knew female beauty.

To live in New York is to constantly consider what beauty is. You are surrounded by it and you are surrounded by people who presume to know it. A native New Yorker once told me that both the beauty and the horror of New York is what it asks of you. Among the many things I felt it was asking of me was to be beautiful, and I was failing.

I saw a woman just the other day, walking down a street in the Village. She had auburn hair swept up in a pompadour. A few tendrils had escaped from underneath her hat, a black tricorn affair fixed in place with two gigantic beaded hat pins that winked in the sun. She wore a green felt peplum coat and brown lace-up hobnail boots; the ruffles of a white petticoat peeked out from underneath her dark skirt.

Oh, and she was walking two poodles, one gray and one black.

I stood transfixed on my own patch of sidewalk. And that is how I saw the woman who intersected her path, a woman who was her opposite in every way, a blanched vegetable in a drab navy coat buttoned to her chin, her face pinched and pale. Her red-rimmed eyes widened as she passed the woman in costume. I couldn't tell from the movement of her thin-lipped mouth whether she was amused or affronted.

For most of my first year here, I would have been the second woman.

Women in New York don't just dress. They don armor. Black is ubiquitous for a reason — it shields, it offers succor, it cancels out the offending form, it lends a kind line to the aging body. In girding myself for the day, I found my hands reaching for the same items over and over — the black boot-cut pants, the suede low-heeled boots, the charcoal-colored boatneck cashmere sweater — as if these garments had amulets sewn into their hems, charms that would leave me somehow better protected. I needed those charms, that protective aura of black. Without them, it was just my undisguised self walking the streets, and I was too new not to feel vulnerable. In my old life, whenever I needed to go somewhere, I jumped in a car. In this life, there was no automotive refuge. When I needed to go somewhere, I joined the parade of people on the streets and in the subways. The beauty and the horror of New York is what it asks of you, my friend said, but she could have added that one of the things it rarely offers is a place to hide.

There would be little hiding in my first year here anyway. I had come to the city to be the cohost of a new show on a new radio network with bestselling author and *Saturday Night Live* star Al Franken. He attracted press, lots of press. On my way to my first meeting, a colleague casually mentioned the documentary crew that would be filming us. He was surprised at my surprise: "No one told you?" By the end of that first week, we were being trailed by two documentary crews, and I had learned to put up a hand if I wanted privacy. So there were film crews and live shots with TV shows and still-photography sessions for publicity photos. This all required makeup, lots and lots of makeup, to be applied by professionals. My favorite in the early days was a big, beefy man with huge hands, a voluble guy who had seen it all: trained under his father, left to teach high school science, and then returned to makeup when the strain of teaching got to be too much. His father had done makeup for *The Honeymooners,* and he had apprenticed under him on that show. Hands that had patted Art Carney's face were now patting down powder on mine. I was thrilled.

I was less thrilled with another makeup artist I met later, a gum-chewing young woman with masses of dark hair held in place by a newsboy cap. She stood back from me with her hands on her hips and scrutinized my face.

"You get a lot of sun when you were younger?" she asked in the sharp tones of the outer boroughs.

No, I —

"Huh. Well, have you thought about trying moisturizer?" she asked next.

Well, yes, as a matter of fact —

"You know, a facial would be a good thing for you," she concluded.

I started to inform her through gritted teeth that I used moisturizing products on a daily basis, received regular facials, and got so little sun in high school that one of my nicknames was "Boo." I was stopped by her sigh of dismay at the work ahead of her, as if someone had brought her the head of John the Baptist on a plate and asked her to get him ready for his close-up.

My friends back home sighed too — with envy. What

American woman weaned on American women's magazines doesn't secretly wonder what would happen if she had the chance for a makeover? What I couldn't explain was how all this attention to my face made me feel worse, highlighted the inadequacy I already felt. My appearance had never been the currency in which I wanted to trade with the world.

Of course, I have felt beautiful in my life, and much of that had to do with context, not cosmetics. When I was married, my husband's inattention to my appearance was a standing joke, and small children in the neighborhood registered my new haircuts or my new outfits before he did. Yet I remember the box of long-stemmed roses he gave me for our last Valentine's Day, a box he inscribed *Pour la belle.* It made me weep — too little too late — and yet, even now, that box sits in the attic of my house in St. Paul. I couldn't bear to throw it away. *Pour la belle:* I was beautiful to him. There is another man in Minnesota, a man who put his arms around me and told me that I was beautiful with such fervor that I disavowed it.

I felt beautiful in that life and with those men because I had a life around me to support that notion. I had friends and community and love, and that, I would argue, is what looks back at you in the mirror. Perhaps that is why some women proclaimed as beauties say they don't see it when they look at their reflection. They have a harmony of skin and flesh and bone, but I had a harmony of all the life that stretched behind me. I was loved, down to the details — the scar on my forehead, the bump on my nose, the freckles I used to pray would go away. I was loved, and I could point to the people who had given me both the worry lines and the laugh lines they found beautiful.

What I needed was someone who knew I wasn't wallpaper.

Lucky me, that in New York I ended up with my new friend John, who runs his own studio where he takes the sketches of designers and turns them into the embodiments of the characters you see onstage. John likes to think of himself as a midwife for the costumes that dot the stages on and off Broadway; I like to think of him as my main Manhattan angel, a midwife to my Manhattan experience.

We were pushed together by friends we held in common, and they described him in such superlatives — So smart! So funny! So much taste! — that I was a little afraid to meet him. And when we were first introduced — it was a year or so before I moved to New York — it was in the glittering salon of a town house, at a crowded holiday party. Kurt Vonnegut was holding forth on one sofa; Uma Thurman was on the stairs. John stood back from the crowd, his tall, lean frame somehow fitting compactly in the elbow-to-elbow crush. He looked forbidding and stern, and I was only later to realize that he hates large parties. He isn't much for small talk; he's a man of real conversation.

We got to know each other when my move to Manhattan became a reality. I had only a few weeks to get my new home in order, and I had decided that I needed a sleeper sofa to accommodate guests. For three brisk January Saturdays in a row, we walked long blocks through the Village and Chelsea, trading our life stories and struggles between stores. We made the acquaintance of every sofa salesman — they were always men — in the district, marveling at how they all seemed to have been cast by David Mamet, muttering out the sides of their mouths about steel springs and iron construction. John won my heart one day at a furniture showroom on Seventh Avenue when he bared his teeth at a young woman who dared to claim the same floor model that I had. She scuttled away. During a trip uptown — Bloomingdale's — for an accompanying armchair, he again came to the rescue when a young married couple began to sit in the chair I was about to buy. While Wife was testing out the cushions, Husband began a search for the price tag. John had already palmed it while I had gone off in search of a salesclerk. At the end of the month, I had a new sofa, a new apartment, and a new friend.

He makes me laugh. A clear plastic drawer underneath his table at the studio holds pieces of fabrics in beiges, tans, and cocoas — skin tones that will be used to line sheer costumes for the stage. The drawer is labeled POUND OF FLESH. I still remember the Sunday afternoon I showed up uninvited at his apartment, carrying two take-out coffees and a cloud of depression. I sat on his sofa and chain-smoked, tears marking runnels down my face: I was too sad, I couldn't stop crying, I was afraid I was going crazy. *I need help,* I told him.

He nodded his head and sipped his coffee.

"Well, Katherine," he said calmly, "I think you're having a perfectly rational reaction to New York."

His design studio is in the heart of the Garment District, on 39th Street between Seventh and Eighth Avenues, one grimy and dusty storefront slammed up against another, a constant collision on the streets of trucks and cabs and dollies, men in delivery uniforms throwing their cigarette butts into the puddles, windows heaped with bolts of fabric, displays of fake fur and fake pearls, gold brocade draped over three kinds of feathers, and signs that promise ALL KINDS OF FABRICS and the WILD WORLD OF TRIM!

He runs his operation with a cutter and four seamstresses, whose places of origin stretch from Dubai to Hong Kong, from Thailand to Ghana. They produce costumes for theater and movies, and I never tire of hearing him talk about his work: the soft-spoken film star in search of sartorial perfection who has had John make him several suits; the heavy-set actress who got tears in her eyes when someone finally made a dress to show off her curves; the armies of stylists who dart in and out of the studio with requests for their A-list clients.

John also produces his own couture for a small roster of private clients. It took me months to work up the nerve, but I dearly wanted a suit made by John, and when the topic was broached, he handled it with his usual tact, sitting me down to make sure I understood what went into the pricing. He gave me a number, I swallowed hard, and then I agreed.

He took me along to a wholesale fabric establishment, and I enjoyed it the way I would a bookstore, trawling up and down the aisles. A bolt of white piqué prompted visions of a smart 1950s-style skirt-and-jacket ensemble. A two-tone taffeta of orange and pink made me long for an exotic cocktail dress. As I went down the aisles, each bolt of fabric was a book with a story to tell and I could read it. John told me later that he was glad I had enjoyed my little romp, because he wasn't taking me back. Ever. I was too distracted, like a kid spun up on sugar let loose in a toy store.

We were several sessions into the suit transaction when I dropped by his studio one afternoon for a fitting. As I walked in, I saw a dress form near the front entrance, a little stout, with wide hips. I stood and surveyed it.

"Is this me?" I asked.

"No," John said, and he pointed to a constellation of dress forms in another corner, armless torsos constructed on poles, with push-pedals to make them taller or shorter. "You're over there. In the red."

As it turns out, I was between the curves of Salma Hayek and the reedy figure of Iman. Their celebrity couldn't hold me, however, as I was too fascinated by the three-dimensional mirror of my own body. There they were, my belly, my breasts, my hips, albeit made of foam and cotton batting. I was looking at my own undisguised self.

"I like her!" I cried, and giving in to my impulses, I flung my arms around her.

The seamstresses — Ying, Pammy, Nina, and Sawatri — began to giggle. John looked up from his table and informed me in dry tones that I was the first customer who had ever hugged her own dress form.

"But she's beautiful," I protested.

"I'm glad you like her," he replied.

I did like her; I still do. I went to visit her the other day. When I walked into John's studio, he was designing patterns for a new clothing line; the seamstresses were working on costumes for a tour of *Oklahoma!* — I saw Aunt Eller's bloomers and a set of black jeans for the cowboys — and Cinderella's fairy godmother had the beginnings of a new gown for a famous department store's holiday window. I walked over to a crowd of dress forms — imagine if you walked into a cocktail party of multiple Venus de Milos — and started looking for mine.

"You're over there," John said. "You have my jacket on."

I was between the actress Kathy Bates and a footman for *Cinderella*. You never know where you will find yourself in this town.

The footman reminded me of the one time I have felt like Cinderella since moving to New York:

I am at the corner of Charles and Hudson Streets, trying to hail a cab on an unseasonably warm June day. I am wearing black chiffon and high heels, rhinestone chandelier earrings, and enough hair spray to blind a child. My ex-husband is going to receive a Tony Award, and I am attending the ceremonies as his guest. If I suck in my stomach, my dress looks just fine, but it's only three in the afternoon, and even in the Village, I feel a little conspicuous in my evening wear.

As I teeter into traffic on my heels, raising my hand for a cab, a woman pulls up in a dark sports-utility vehicle. She is stopping for the traffic light, but she looks down at me, smiles, and leans out her window.

"You look beautiful!" she cries out.

"Oh, thanks," I say, with heartfelt relief. "I really needed to hear that."

"Where you going?"

"The Tonys!"

"Well, you look great!" she says.

The light changes and she moves on, leaving me laughing in her wake. What is it that my friend told me? The beauty and the horror of New York is what it asks of you. And right now, I feel like it is asking me to be grateful. And I am. I feel beautiful.

Hunger

I'M SEEING MY FRIEND DAVID for dinner. When I first knew him he was a rumpled writer in a sweatshirt who wrote for an alternative paper in Minneapolis. Now he's a reporter for the *New York Times,* and he directs me to meet him at a Portuguese restaurant in the Village. He shows up in a sleek black-wool jacket, with a cell phone buzzing like an angry insect. He apologizes: he's on deadline and he might have to take some calls.

"Try the clams," he says as he reaches for the phone. "'Scuse me."

David is prone to pronouncements. The last time we met for dinner, maybe six years ago, I was auditioning for a National Public Radio show and he was the editor of a weekly paper in Washington, DC. I was newly divorced, and while we ate, he tried to sketch out what life would be like for me in the nation's capital.

"You get this job and you'll never date again," he said. "I'm serious. This town is hell on women. You see the ugliest guy and he's with a beautiful woman. You. Will. Never. Date. Again."

I never had the chance to test his hypothesis. I didn't get the job.

Now, here in New York, I'm looking forward to talking to him, the way I look forward to talking to anyone who knew the old me. I have been here only a few months, and I want someone to tell me that I can survive this move, that I will feel like myself again soon. There is little fat in a conversation with David; his candor gets regular exercise, so I am not altogether surprised when he issues a challenge instead of offering a bromide.

"You'll make it here if you're hungry," he declares. Then he looks at me with his eyebrows raised. "Now we'll see how hungry you are."

The phone buzzes and he takes another call.

Oh, I want to tell him, don't worry. I'm hungry. I'm hungry for all sorts of things. New York has a way of sharpening your appetite.

Soon after I move to New York, I begin making pilgrimages to a butcher shop on Bleecker Street, an old-fashioned place with a wooden storefront and a red-and-white-striped awning.

The name of the shop — Ottomanelli and Sons — is spelled out in wooden letters. A large plate-glass window displays huge uncut hams of prosciutto, fresh duck legs, whole dressed rabbits, and smoked beef tongues. A small sign promises homemade lamb sausage for $4.00 a pound. When you walk inside, a faint whiff of packinghouse greets your nose. It's an agreeable scent, the smell of the possible. I am always happy at a good butcher shop, the way woodworkers are happy when they are at a well-stocked lumberyard. For me, the butcher shop is a place of potential.

There are all sorts of ways to construct a life, and one of the ways I make mine is with food. Ottomanelli's is run by five brothers, and after a while I can tell them apart: the one who looks as though he might have been a boxer; the one with the broad face and smile; the quiet, tall one. In my efforts to insinuate myself as a regular, I go in at least once a week. I buy lilliputian roasts — "just enough for me and some leftovers" — and happily answer questions about how I might cook the roast in question. The Ottomanelli waiting on me wants to know if I have ever tried basting the veal with white wine instead of red? Sure, he says, some fresh thyme is a great idea. Then he wraps the roast in white paper, pats the top of it, and says, "OK, I'll be over around seven."

This makes me smile. I love flirting with butchers, an age-old arrangement that sweetens the transactions of blood and meat. Years ago, I was wheeling my grocery cart past the meat counter at a market in St. Paul when the young man with whom I often did business leaned over the glass case and half-hissed his come-on.

"Hey! Wanna goose?"

To tell you the truth, I wasn't exactly sure what he meant. I stopped.

He looked exasperated. "Do you want a goose?" he said slowly, holding aloft a pale yellow bird, about ten pounds. It was only twenty-four hours before its sell-by date, and if I didn't take it, he'd have to throw it out. He was offering it to me.

Reader, I took the bird. I roasted it with apples. I was thrilled with that night's demonstration to my then husband of my skills of procurement and thrift.

I also used to haunt a small old-fashioned grocery, dark with floor-to-ceiling shelves. The clerks went after your canned goods for you with a movable ladder. It wasn't hard to imagine that F. Scott Fitzgerald's family used to shop there: the place had stayed alive only through delivery and custom orders for the carriage trade in the wealthy nearby neighborhood of Crocus Hill, with its prosperous-looking houses that ruled the bluff overlooking downtown.

I frequented the place because it fit the narrative in my head, the story I was telling myself about my marriage and the home I was establishing. It was the only place I knew of where you could buy lamb kidneys, a delicacy that was a favorite of my husband's. When the butcher started setting them aside for me, I beamed with pride at this example of my good housewifery. After I had made several such purchases, the butcher told me that only one other customer asked for the little paper parcels of kidneys tied up with string. Her dog loved them.

Oh, I said flatly. I'm buying them for my husband.

In those early married days, I referred to myself as a matron-in-training. I collected linens and place cards and ceramic knife rests, I created elaborate dinners for fourteen, serving the salad *after* the entrée and with a cheese course before the fruit and dessert. It was all, as the French say, *très propre*. Now I'm buying miniature roasts for one and slowly amassing a library of take-out menus. I wonder sometimes what it would be like if one of the butchers really came over for dinner. Back when I was training to be a matron, this wasn't my idea of how it was going to be.

It's hard for me not to weave together food and love, and food stories with love stories. The story of my married life began on a Minneapolis theater set, a mock-up of a Parisian café, and it began when V asked me to dance at a cast party. He was not yet forty, a native of Paris born in the postwar years, the only surviving son of a French general and his wife, an architect who finished his studies to please his parents and then abandoned his profession to follow his real love: theater. That love had led him, improbably, to Minnesota, where he was one of four founders of a French-American theater troupe. I was twenty-five, a young reporter for the newspaper in St. Paul, still working weekends and covering cops, and I had an unrequited passion for another man; I had been mooning about for weeks, and I had gone to V's show to shake off my gloom.

We danced well together, moving in step over the black-and-white tiles of the faux café floor, and he offered to show me the rest of the theater, an old vaudeville house. I think we were in the costume shop when we first kissed. We were on the second floor, wrapped up in dusty velvet curtains, when we heard our names echoing off the walls below: our friends were looking for us, to say good night. We kept mum. Eventually there was silence, and we crept downstairs to the lobby, where plates of food still sat on a table. I remember tearing off chunks of bread from a baguette and the rough taste of a meat pâté on my tongue; I remember red wine poured into a paper cup. Suddenly, I was hungry.

At some point in our courtship, V boasted that he could kill a rabbit, dress it, and then make terrine. I believed him, despite the fact that he was living without a kitchen. He lived in the West Bank neighborhood of Minneapolis, renting a single room in an old brick building by the railroad tracks, on a deserted street where nearly every other structure had been torn down. His building was slated for demolition as well, but it was close to the old vaudeville theater where he performed and to the bar where all the actors gathered for dollar beers. His room held a futon and a boom box for his beloved jazz tapes, and we sat there many nights, listening to Coltrane or Monk, smoking Gauloises and drinking water.

He had no phone, so if I wanted to see him at the last minute, I had to drive by his building and look to see if his light was on. Then I would stand out in the street, calling his name.

I had the grace to feel faintly ridiculous. But I did it. On winter nights, as I shouted for him, my breath escaped my lips in cold white wisps. His own voice was deep and throaty, with a French accent as thick as syrup. I joked to friends that I could listen to him read the phone book — "The white pages!" — and never tire of hearing the timbre of his voice. I was in love. I was hungry for identity, and association with him seemed to offer it forth.

So I'm standing near the door of Ottomanelli's, waiting for one of the butchers to cut up some lamb shoulder. We've just had a thoroughly satisfactory conversation about the lamb ragu I want to make, and while he works, I study a photograph from years ago of all the butchers assembled on the sidewalk in front of the store. I busy myself with matching the younger men in the photo with the white-haired men behind the counter. Then I hear a voice calling out from the street.

"Hey! Hey you!"

I look around. It's a Saturday afternoon, and at the moment I am the only customer.

"HEY!"

The voice is insistent. I look outside. A red-faced, white-haired man is leaning out the driver's-side door of a navy pickup truck. His eyes lock on mine.

"Tell 'em I'm here," he says, gesturing with a cigar. "I'm here for a pickup. They're expecting me. The name's Van Perry."

I swivel on my feet to the glass case and the line of white-coated butchers. I relay the information.

"Awwww, jeez," says the short, skinny one. "What does he think I am, a valet?"

"Hey, come ON!" the man bellows. "I can't park heah. I gotta move. Tell them to HURRY IT UP!"

I don't have to tell them anything, the butchers can hear every word. One sighs and, shaking his head, pushes through the swinging metal doors to the back, muttering, "Every-one's in a hurry, everyone's in a hurry."

A red double-decker tour bus begins to squeeze its way down Bleecker, exhaust belching, engine wheezing. By now, other customers have joined me in the store and we all watch as the bus approaches the Van Perry truck, close enough to shear off the passenger's-side mirror. This could get inter-esting.

"HEY! It should be ready! I called! I got nowhere to park!"

The butcher cutting my lamb turns to me, purposefully unruffled by the shouting. He asks, "You want the bone?"

I nod — I might make lamb stock — and turn to see that the man with the cigar now has half his body out the truck window. He's still screaming at me and the butchers.

"HEY, C'MON! Can you hear me in there?"

"Jeez, what an asshole," a man says to his female companion. They are ordering one of the specials of the day, a cut of lean beef for $5.99 a pound.

"HEY!" I hear again and wonder why I have been singled out as the messenger of wrath. I begin to inch over toward the freezer cases in the back of the store, out of the sight line of Mr. Belligerent. The tall butcher — the one I think must have played baseball — flashes me one of his quiet grins.

"Standing away from the door, now, huh? Whatsa matta, you don't want to do our curbside?"

"Sure," I say. "I'll wear roller skates."

When my friends come to visit, I always tell them that, for the price of a sidewalk-vendor hot dog, they can have dinner and a show — the people on the street here are that amusing. Or, as in this case, you can get your weekend entertainment for the price of some lamb shoulder. The Ottomanellis need someone to do curbside deliveries on roller skates? What they don't realize is that, for the right amount of lamb shoulder, or skirt steak or venison sausage, I would probably do it.

Until I met V, I had little desire to cook, a symptom of my misguided interpretation of feminism. I had feared that I would be chained to a lifetime of culinary drudgery if I learned how to wield a wooden spoon. But V was from Paris and his compatriots in the theater either were French or had studied in France. They loved to cook. Each Monday they would gather in a friend's kitchen, a noisy, rambunctious, inventive school of cooks. It was there that I first saw a tarte tatin that didn't come from a bakery. I watched as one actor assembled a potato galette and another made slits in a leg of lamb, into which he could insert slivers of garlic. The first night I was invited to join this kitchen of players, I picked up a paring knife and a head of garlic with nonchalance, as if I knew what I was doing. My clumsy hands gave me away soon enough, and one of the actors gave me a kind look and took the knife and garlic away from me. "Why don't you sit down and have a glass of wine?" she suggested.

I resolved then and there to learn how to cook, really cook. My self-tutorial took place in the kitchen of my rickety apartment on Avon Street in St. Paul, part of a once-comfortable sixplex that had been further divided and subdivided for profit. My three rooms on the third floor were the truncated front end of a railroad-style apartment: I reaped the large, airy sitting room and its porch with fat wooden railings. I had a grand view of the roofs of the robber-baron mansions a block away. For this glory, I put up with a bedroom that was nothing more than a grandiose hallway, since the only way to get to the kitchen was to walk past my bed and bureau. When I moved in, I had put up new wallpaper in the kitchen, a large plaid in primary colors. I had also put up modern white, open shelving, which contrasted with the original features that were still intact: a Hoosier cabinet painted white and an old-fashioned kitchen sink with its own porcelain draining board. The floors sloped, and you could tell where my friends and I had failed to match the lines of the wallpaper, but I loved that room and what it represented: the first strong lines of a story I was writing each day.

A copy of *Joy of Cooking* that I had received as a gift in college served as my guide, along with a beloved paperback collection of recipes called *A Cookbook for Poor Poets*. I had my share of disasters, usually when I deviated from the instructions. Note: cream cheese with raw garlic is not a big hit as a spread for crudités. Once, I tried to puree pumpkin for a pie and hit the "mix" button on the blender without remembering to put the lid back on.

Disaster of another sort happened when, after nearly eight months together, V and I broke up. He would later become my husband — and then my ex-husband — but I wasn't to know any of that. All I knew was that we had parted and I thought it was forever. We had made our good-byes on a park bench, sitting glumly on the cold wood, looking at the dead March grass that edged Lake of the Isles in Minneapolis.

He wasn't the man for me, he explained. I wanted to get married — here I wanted to cry out in indignation, "No I don't!" but it was true — and he was already married to the theater. He told me he would make a bad husband.

Oh, how I hated him for saying that. I hissed like a goose, retorting that he could leave me behind if he wanted, but he would be lonely with only a theater for a spouse. "When you're old and alone in your little house in France," I told him, "my children will send you cookies because they feel sorry for you."

I was not about to let a missing man get in the way of my dogged march through my cookbooks. I had set my heart on conquering a recipe for béchamel sauce, so I labored one Sunday afternoon, going after my version of the Great White Sauce. Heartbreak is a terrible sous-chef. Fat, hot tears plopped on the pages of my copy of *Joy of Cooking*. I snuffled as I stirred the roux. At one point I gave up, putting my flour-dusted hands on the enamel-coated countertop of the Hoosier cabinet and leaning into the cupboards for a good wail.

I haven't tried to make béchamel sauce since.

A friend and I joke that sex with a man is one thing, but if we cook for him, THEN he had better call us the next day. You want intimacy? I offer you my shellfish stew, made with a base of red zinfandel and modified from an old *Silver Palate Cookbook;* or my chicken-liver mousse, from an old Jacques Pépin recipe. I made the shellfish stew one night for a new love in Minnesota, carefully ladling it into a shallow soup bowl, sprinkling chopped Italian parsley over the steaming broth. I had slices of baguette and a ripe cheese on the table, and a glass of red wine to marry with the soup. He rubbed his hands, remarked on how good everything looked, and then used his fingers to fish a throat lozenge out of his mouth, depositing it on the side of his plate. I thought, *This affair might not work.*

When I moved to New York, I wanted to take my kitchen with me — all of it. I could not imagine life without the fish poacher and the stockpot. What about that set of pink luncheon dishes I had found at an antiques mall? They were perfect when I hosted bridal or baby showers. Then there was the berry bowl I had found in France, a porcelain colander that rested on a matching plate.

I was dissuaded by a friend who helped me pack. When she saw what I was intending to take, she downloaded the dimensions of my Manhattan kitchen — an open galley of two cupboards and an oven — and waved the computer printout in front of me, repeatedly, until I relented. To her great amusement, however, I did insist on bringing the leaves to my dining room table. I live in two rooms in less than six hundred feet, but I have the leaves, and if need be, I can seat fourteen.

If anything demonstrates how little I understood what my new life was going to be like, perhaps it's the table leaves. I have never sat more than four in this apartment, and even that has been a rare occasion. I was trying to move the life I knew — a circle of friends, a table of plenty, evenings of laughter and neighbors and dinner parties — but I had moved only the objects, not the people. By the end of my first year in New York, I suffered from a grim mood for which I coined my own disorder: displacement dysphasia. I would be walking down a street and suddenly the oddness of my surroundings would hit me with a painful clarity. This wasn't home. These weren't my streets. What was I doing here?

One February evening, as dusk began to fall, I found that I couldn't walk, that with every dragging step I had this sudden fear of the sidewalk rising up to swallow me. I stopped dead on Hudson Street, and the other pedestrians swarmed around me like water diverting around a rock. I forced myself to the closest wall and leaned against it, brushing my hands over the rough brick to prove to myself that I was really here.

I can mark my marriage by what we ate. The first summer I went to visit V's extended family, we gathered by a river for an outdoor feast at an old mill his cousin had turned into a country home. I ate so much goat cheese that one of his cousins turned to me, leaned in close, and in mock solemnity whispered, "We will get you a goat." I picked up on the French habit of moderation after that. V and I were married on an island in the middle of the Mississippi River in Minneapolis, and we served a buffet that included roasted lamb, haricots verts, and two kinds of wedding cake — a traditional American cake and a French *croquembouche,* a tower of little cream puffs melded together with caramel. My mother-in-law thought the lamb was dry.

When we bought our first house, we held a Thanksgiving dinner for thirty-four, covering the jerry-rigged tables with jacquard cloths and spreading out every piece of china we owned. A few years later, when V opened a show in New Haven the week of Thanksgiving, I toted a turkey roaster on a plane as my carry-on luggage so we could cook together.

I never saw him kill a rabbit but can attest to his making a fine terrine. When I think of our years together, I think of our nightly cribbage games after he came home from the theater, of the way he would sing to me on airplanes when the turbulence made me grip the armrests in fear — and of his braised lamb shanks, the deft touch he had with glazed carrots.

Once, he had failed to show up as promised to help me pack up our belongings for a move to a house we had just purchased. In a fit of pique, I had thrown away a bag of groceries rather than transferring it all by myself. A tin of foie gras had been in the bag. When he finally came home and realized what I had done, his face assumed a mask of tragedy. An hour later, we were rooting through the Dumpster at the corner convenience store where I had tossed the bag. When a curious driver in the parking lot turned his high beams on us, I was pinned in the ersatz spotlight. V was hoisting me by the knees so I could reach into the giant garbage bin. "It's OK!" I yelled. "We're just looking for foie gras."

It says everything to me that, the year we separated, we couldn't bear to cook Thanksgiving and went to a friend's house instead, where V glowered at me from across the table. After a decade of marriage, I had decided that he was right, that he was married to the theater before he was married to me. But he had decided that I was right, that he might end up alone without me, and he wanted us to stay together. I can't tell you what we ate during those weeks of separation and divorce, but I remember that the food tasted like ash.

★　　★　　★

Not long after the displacement dysphasia first strikes, I meet a friend at a Midtown hotel for tea. We sit at a little table in a mezzanine bar, watch as the jacketed waiter brings our white ceramic pots of Earl Grey. I can feel my depression slink in like a pair of silent gray hounds, the pads of their feet barely making a sound on the thick carpet, their silky limbs making not a rustle as they fold themselves at my feet. I go home early. The dogs get up and follow me.

To banish the dogs, to root myself back in the world, to show myself I still exist, I cook. My dictum in New York becomes "When in doubt, roast a chicken." I'm not referring to the doubt you suffer when you aren't sure what you should eat. I'm talking about existential despair, the gloom that gnaws at you as you question your place in the universe. Roasting a chicken becomes a ritual. I have few memories of actually eating these birds, but preparing them sates another kind of hunger. The smells alone start to heal me — the way rosemary tickles my nose with pine, the almost floral sharpness of a cut lemon. With each deliberate motion of my hands, I am willing myself to the next.

Most days, I like to think that I am constructing a life, but on these bleak evenings, I am settling for an hour and the hour after that and the hour after that. I am hungry for a rooted life, and cooking staves off the hunger pangs. These small kitchen acts are like the tracery I did as a child, when I would place a piece of translucent paper over a beloved illustration and carefully, carefully trace with my pencil. Now, I am tracing acts of sustenance.

When-in-Doubt Chicken

1 chicken, around 5 pounds, preferably organic
softened butter
salt and pepper
2 large carrots and 2 leeks, chopped in 1-inch pieces
handful of garlic cloves
1 sprig rosemary
1 lemon, cut in half
white wine or chicken stock (2 cups or to taste)
white vermouth (optional)

Preheat your oven to 425 degrees. Rinse the chicken and then pat dry with paper towels. Take a nice helping of the butter and massage it into the skin of the chicken. Salt and pepper the bird. Sprinkle carrots, leeks, and garlic cloves over the bottom of a Dutch oven or roasting pan; they will function as your roasting rack. Put rosemary and lemon in the cavity of the bird. Slosh some chicken stock or white wine in the bottom of the pan.

Roast the bird, uncovered, for 15 minutes. Reduce heat to 350 degrees. Figure 15 minutes per pound.

Add more stock or white wine every 20 minutes. After the allotted time is up, pierce the chicken with a large fork. If the juices run clear, it's done. Put the bird to rest on a carving board while you remove the vegetables with a slotted spoon. (These will be the best carrots you have eaten in a long time.) Put them in a small bowl and cap with foil to keep them warm.

Then pour in a large splash of white vermouth (optional) or wine into the pan, turn up the heat, and stir while you reduce the sauce. Once you think you have boiled off the alcohol, pour the sauce into a separator to reduce the amount of fat you'll be eating. By now, your chicken is ready to carve.

My favorite sign at the Greenmarket in Union Square is at a tiny booth that sells tarts and cakes. ATTENTION NEW YORKERS, it reads, EGGS ARE NOT DAIRY. In case there are any misunderstandings, the posting is illustrated with pint-size drawings of cows and chickens. By July, the corner fruit stand is selling both yellow and white peaches. A stern admonition in block letters begs customers not to touch the fruit unless they're going to buy it because it bruises so easily. Nonetheless, the table is covered with fruit mottled by fingerprints, and every push has released a little peach perfume — it is heavenly to stand there. By August, the radishes look like rubies; and the white-tipped French breakfast variety are especially beautiful. The carrots are in jewel tones too: purple, russet, yellow, and orange. I buy them, along with the multihued stalks of rainbow chard and the rough-edged leaves of wild arugula. I buy blackberries too, but only after walking back and forth past the lone stand that offers them, arguing with myself about the price.

Once I have gathered my zinnias and radishes and tomatoes and basil and peaches, I walk my bike over to the gladiola stand, a raffish-looking operation on the edges of the market, with buckets and buckets of rough-cut glads that have been hauled out of the back of a paneled truck. I buy two bunches and then begin the delicate operation of balancing my purchases on the bike. Heavy goods such as fingerling potatoes and radishes go in first. Medium-weight items are wedged in my backpack. I thread the glads through the large openings of the basket mesh, the long lines of blossoms sticking out at perpendicular angles like floral versions of cat whiskers. Easily decimated produce — such as the aforementioned blackberries — then rest gently on top of the basket, held in place by smaller bouquets of flowers.

Then I clap on my straw hat and commence the ride home, wobbling a bit at first from the weight at the basket end of the bike. I look ridiculous. I don't care. Even this early on a Saturday, negotiating Union Square traffic is precarious, and I pray that people take note of my basket of gladiolas and give me a wide berth. I emit a ritual sigh of relief when I leave the traffic-choked blocks and get back onto the residential streets that function for me the way alleys would, although these instead are lined with elegant old brownstones. I beam as I skim down the streets, the gladiolas bobbing in front of me, the facades of town houses unspooling on either side of me as in a film.

One Saturday, trying to cross Seventh Avenue, I'm forced by construction and traffic to continue pedaling amid a herd of taxis. I notice that one cab has pulled even with me, the better for the driver to lean over toward the passenger window and let loose a barrage of invective that ends with, let's just say, a strong endorsement that I get off the street.

Oh, and there is an action he would desire I take against my mother.

The gladiolas bob as I pedal. I tell him to go and do the same to his mother.

I am finally able to make a right turn back into the placid, narrow, tree-lined lanes of town houses and churches and cafés that make up my neighborhood. I am passing an Episcopal church on Waverly Street when a woman about my age sees me and clasps her hands in delight. She leans forward from her waist to yell in a distinct New York accent, "You look like a picture!" The phonetic spelling of that, by the way, would be "Yuh luk like a pikcha!" It has been a long time since I have heard sweeter words.

Landscapes

I HAVE MORE LIGHT than anyone I know in New York. I live now in two rooms in an eighth-floor aerie in the Village, no small feat for a woman who was so house-proud. The main room has windows on three walls, and it is this embarrassment of light and view that makes the trade seem almost fair, especially on the evenings when I'm home for sunset and I can sit on one of my tall kitchen chairs and watch the pink, pink light pour into my apartment. The light makes me feel rich. I think maybe it has made me greedy. I feel a sort of protective avarice about the light that floods this place; I'm just lucky that it comes every day, without my asking.

When I look west, I see the Hudson River and its gradations of color throughout the day, from a cerulean blue that reflects the morning sky to a darkening slate at dusk. In the summer, the stiff white triangles of sailboats slip by in the distance, and at night, cruise ships and elegant pleasure yachts outlined in tiny lights move downriver at a stately pace. All year long, I hear the moaning cries of barges, my river chorus. I am across the water from the lights of Hoboken and an old ferry terminal with the name LACKAWANNA emblazoned across its span in stout white letters. "Lackawanna" is Algonquin for "where the streams meet," but the name has this elegiac note to me, something that connotes a great and wistful longing: lack and want, Lackawanna. I've had my moments of Lackawanna looking across that river.

The latest addition to my view is a blurry reflection of the Empire State Building, a ghost structure hovering in the tall glass of one of the towers that Richard Meier built on the Hudson. The Meier building wasn't here when I moved in and it has eaten up part of my river view, a loss that connects me to other New Yorkers, a stamp in my Manhattan passport. That reflection of the Empire State Building is an addition garnered from a subtraction.

I look south and I see the half-moon arches of the windows in the old Federal Archive Building down the street. I've been told that I would have had a view of the World Trade Center towers as well, but it's not an absence that registers for me. What strikes me instead are the stories I hear from any New Yorker who visits my apartment and stops, eyes craning south, to tell me of the view I would have had; they can still see it, I know, from the way their eyes rest on emptiness but somehow register recognition. I often hear, unprompted, where my visitor was that day — what he was doing, what she saw, the dreams that still haunt.

I don't look south that often. If my eyes aren't drawn to the river, then I look east, out a bank of floor-to-ceiling windows, past my tiny terrace to the roofscape that unfolds before me, gables and cornices and chimneys, onion-topped domes of ventilation stacks jutting up into the air like Russian churches, stout wooden barrels of water towers perched on spindly legs. As beautiful as the river is, the east is my favorite view, the direction in which I first began to fall in love with my new landscape.

It is snowing. Snow softens the outlines here, renders the sooty blacks and grays into charcoals and creams. The swirling snow becomes a scrim and all the illuminated windows of the surrounding buildings turn into glowing bars of topaz. My own window into that scene becomes a portal then, and I can close my eyes and open them to London or Paris and not be surprised. I remember the first night I saw, really saw, my winter roofscape. I had padded out into the living room because I couldn't sleep, and the beauty of the storm caught my eyes. I gathered an old afghan and settled into a chair to watch. If I had listened, I might have heard a small snick, the sound of my heart sliding back into place.

When do you know you're home? When do you claim a landscape as your own? When I was a child, we drove out to the Illinois countryside an hour or so away from Moline nearly every other weekend to visit my maternal grandmother. I can close my eyes and summon the moving picture

I observed from the back of the family sedan: rows and rows of corn and soybeans ticking past the passenger window like bicycle spokes. I can still feel the rhythm and bump of the car wheels on those two-lane asphalt roads. In summers, we would stop at small farm stands and buy muskmelon for my father; in the fall, we'd stop to buy wreaths of bittersweet with their flame-orange berries for my mother. I am not a country child. I don't know how to husk corn or feed cattle, but ask me where I was raised and the first picture that comes to mind is those lines of green against the dark soil; I can hear the mild, knowing commentary of my parents, both farm kids, from the front seat. I wouldn't know an ear of field corn from sweet corn, but I knew, from them, to look for stalks that were "knee-high by the Fourth of July." The sheer repetition of that journey and those pictures engraved it on my brain and then, I suspect, on my heart.

My first moment of communion with the landscape of Minnesota came outside an ice-fishing shack on two-hundred-square-mile Lake Mille Lacs, near the center of the state. Four of us — a poet, a real estate agent, a computer guru, and I — were ensconced in a six-holer, our poles rigged up with belled jigs so we could hear if there were any bites in the water below. The poet was an old hand at ice fishing on this lake, and we had stopped by her brother's shack earlier in the day; she navigated her way through the addresses as if she were in a suburban cul-de-sac. A decade ago ice fishing was still mostly considered a man's sport, and we were full of mirth when we heard a heavy hand on the door and a beery voice demanding entrance. The poor angler who had gotten his ice-shack address wrong could barely disguise his incredulity at the sight of four women with cards and poles.

Whenever I told this story later, listeners would lean in and say, "What happened next?" My answer was always the same: "Catch and release."

During a lull in the card game later that night, I stepped outside. There is something beautiful about looking at a village of tiny shacks affixed to frozen water, a wind-chill township that emerges only when the ice is firm enough and it's too cold to do much else. There is something too about the ice as that frozen line of delineation between one world and the next: you look down that dark hole, hear the slap of the water, and wonder what's really there.

That night, white pinpoints of stars speckled the big, dark, open sky. A stretch of silver-blue frozen lake rolled out in front of me, and the shadowed contours of the huts dotted the lake for miles. When you're on top of a big frozen lake like that, you hear creaks and snaps, the sound of the ice shifting its burden. Although I had lived in the state for years, I had never really seen it, not like that, and I fell a little in love with winter that night.

Before I left Minnesota for New York, I wanted to see that vista again, hear that sound. So I traveled north with a friend to an inn on the Grand Portage Indian Reservation, a small and compact house a stone's throw from Lake Superior, tucked just miles from the Canadian border. We went cross-country skiing during the day, moving down gentle swells of snow among the birches and pines. At night, we ran out of the Finnish sauna, our skin boiled red, and then plopped ourselves into a hot tub built on a wooden stand surrounded by firs. The steam curled about our faces, and if we were quiet, we could hear the aching, long groans of the lake ice.

I wanted to take that sound with me. I was sure I would never hear such quietude again. I soon discovered, however, that there is a Manhattan version of that sound, if only in the first hours after a heavy snowfall, when a sort of ease takes over the city, and the snow muffles more than noise. In the Village, near Union Square, people trudge in thick boots down the middle of Broadway because, well, they can. The calm in the air feels plush.

I had returned from my sojourn in northern Minnesota only recently when I encountered my first Manhattan snowstorm, and I walked through the near-deserted white-blanketed streets with something like wonder. I had never seen New York so composed. I ended up in the wake of two women tramping down a sidewalk and overheard one of them say, "So you take the moose when it's still warm in the middle . . ." and I was shocked that the petite figure in a parka in front of me was a hunter, and such an experienced one. *You just never know in this city,* I told myself. A few blocks later, I realized I had overheard a culinary conversation: she was talking about a *mousse.*

The snow lined the days that I spent looking for a place to live. I hadn't brought my Minnesota-proof snow boots to the city. After one day of stamping and stomping through some knee-high drifts, I looked at my red, frozen feet and considered the ignominy of getting frostbite in lower Manhattan. Still, the snow felt welcome to me, the same way my heart lifted a bit when I stood in front of a brownstone and watched as a silver-haired man strode past carrying cross-country skis.

"Excuse me!" I called out. "I'm moving here from Minnesota. Where do people ski here?"

He didn't break pace for his answer, just turned his head and boomed out, "Central Park!"

While I still haven't skied in the park, I have skied up and down the path along the Hudson River. I felt self-conscious the first time I tucked the ungainly skis under one arm and left my building. I paused for a moment outside, and I could feel my face heat up. The skis made me feel a little silly and conspicuous. Then I reminded myself: I live in a neighborhood with film actors, transvestite prostitutes, pot-smoking reactionaries, and a long string of fetish shops. With so much else going on, why would anyone bother to turn and study me?

It's easy to look back now and see that the snow represented a constant between my old life and my new life. Everything else I encountered that January as I looked for a home had a sheen of the exotic to it: dark and tiny apartments that reminded me of bento boxes for a Japanese lunch, closets outfitted as kitchens, beds that folded into the wall, and fourth-floor walk-ups where the stairs warped so severely that you climbed at a double-tilt.

This was not how I envisioned home. Home was my 1914 Prairie-style house in St. Paul, with its mullioned windows and multiple bedrooms, the garden where I had trained roses to climb and coaxed a cassis bush to life. I thought of the warning a friend had given me when he heard of my plans to move East: "I don't know," he said, his mouth making a grim line. "You're such a nester. People don't build many nests there."

My hopes lifted when I found the secret garden. The apartment was on the ground floor of a building on Perry Street, just a block or so from the river. But it wasn't the location or even the large rooms or the open kitchen that drew me back for repeated viewings. It was the garden, an expanse of grass and tile and pots and planters and walls that even under the snow looked bigger than some of the apartments I had viewed. When I looked out the sliding glass doors that led to the garden, I felt at home, and I paused so long at those doors each time I went to visit that my nose and hands left little greasy smudges on the glass. I could have told you where I would plant hollyhocks, where I would drape honeysuckle, where I would install a clutch of hosta and Solomon's seal. The apartment was too expensive, but with the garden, the rent sounded like the necessary investment for my survival. I would have a secret Manhattan garden. I grew giddy at the prospect.

A no-nonsense friend saved me. At my request, she zipped down in a cab on her lunch hour to look at the place. She was kind, but brisk: the garden was too dark. She wanted to see the other apartment on the short list, a smaller place a third of the way up a twenty-two-story building, also close to the river. It was less chic, it was more affordable, it had no secret garden.

When we walked in, though, the light hit us. On my previous visit, the sky had been overcast. Now, the sunlight bounced off the white walls of the empty unit, streaming in from three walls of windows. My friend, a woman who had lived between St. Paul and Manhattan most of her life, looked at me and shook her head. "Oh, Katherine," she said, "you won't be sorry if you take this. You'll be happy because of the light."

She's right. I may live in a small space, but the light makes it larger. Day or night, the sky extends my two rooms into the city beyond. My bedroom holds an armoire, bookcases, an antique bed frame, and a tiny computer desk; more important, it has a window that gives me a view of the Chrysler Building. As I type these words, the Deco scallops at the top are barely visible through the fog, but most nights they shine for me like the display window at Tiffany's. I'm still nesting; I'm just nesting higher up.

The city has taught me to view landscape differently. The first spring I was here, it rained incessantly. I was walking home one night, down 34th Street at rush hour, traversing from Park Avenue to Seventh Avenue and past the landmarks that told me I was getting closer to my subway stop, past the Empire State Building, past Herald Square, past Macy's. I looked around and realized that I could have been in the currents of some urban ocean, the undulating lines of pedestrians moving like schools of fish through the wet and the deep blue dusk, illuminated by store windows and neon, punctuated by the revolving lights of darting police cars and ambulances. Town cars idled in long lines at the curbside, their smoked windows glistening like mackerels.

Sometimes, I think of the city as this instrument I can play simply by walking down its sidewalks, every step setting off a trip wire that prompts the street scene, the encounter, the overheard conversation that is then built into my vision of the landscape here. Or maybe Manhattan is more like a player piano, where the keys lift up and plunk down whether your hands dance over them or not. However it is played, the tune is something to which I've become accustomed. I find these little moments beautiful:

"I need to make water," a tired-looking man tells me outside the D'Agostino grocery on Greenwich Street. He's in a worn coat and he's hopping back and forth, waiting to sell his bag of aluminum cans to the store manager. "I've been waiting," he says again, "and I need to make water."

At the corner of Sixth Avenue and 14th Street, a fat man sits on a low stool and dully intones, "Magic mouse, magic mouse, magic mouse," as a little toy with a long tail scurries in a loop around his meaty closed fist. He looks up at people through unkempt, curly brown hair.

"Do you believe in God or do you BELIEVE God?" yells a kid with a Latino accent at the tunnel to the A-train platform at Times Square. "'Cuz there's a big difference."

It's after-hours at my bank branch, and a woman about my age opens the door for me to the outer lobby cash machine. She looks me right in the eye. "They should have a guard here. This place is dangerous. It was robbed this morning. Yeah, at gunpoint." Having dispatched her opinion, she walks on.

Such people speak directly to me with little or no provocation: a nod at the fine day, a smile at a shared obstacle such as a closed door. In her memoir *Speaking with Strangers,* Mary Cantwell describes the need of New Yorkers to talk: "Words pile up behind their closed mouths like clothes that have been crammed into a too-small suitcase." She recommends that if you really want to hear those words, you can ride the bus.

Near my one-year anniversary of moving to Manhattan, I board a bus line a block from my apartment with the intention of eventually getting down to Battery Park on the southernmost tip of the island. From there, I want to travel all the way to the opposite end, sitting by a bus window so that my eyes can record the landscape.

It takes me two different buses before I am in view of the Staten Island Ferry and Battery Park, and when I leave the second, I ask the stone-faced driver for some advice.

"All you need is time," he replies, and then he turns to scold me. "Well. You should have told me what you wanted to do when you came on."

Then he gives me a string of route numbers to follow, a plan I soon abandon, deciding instead to rely on the kindness of other bus drivers. It's not a bad plan. When they hear what I want to do, most of the drivers laugh.

I say I want to record the landscape, but I'm drawn by what's going on inside the bus as well. I observe my community. On a bus going up Sixth Avenue, just crossing from Tribeca into Soho, a middle-aged black woman in a sensible coat and a bright blue beret brings out her knitting, silently working some red yarn with her needles. The bus is full of Italian tourists, one woman with copper hennaed hair and large dark glasses talking into her cell phone, *"Va bene! Va bene!"* A blond American woman in a fur coat and a shearling cap with earflaps sits behind her, trying to apply red lipstick. She pauses for the different lurches and bumps of the bus.

At 12th Street and Sixth Avenue a woman in a black plush coat with a bright magenta scarf stops to observe the knitting woman. "Do you need to know my size?" she asks before stepping off. By the time we are past the Garment District and heading into Midtown, the woman in the fur coat is deep in conversation with the Italian, who has been foolish enough to answer in the affirmative when Fur Coat asks, "Are you visiting?"

"You are!" I hear. "Are you from Italy? I thought so. My brother, he teaches Italian at State College in Pennsylvania. Have you heard of it? STATE COLLEGE. I love your jeans. Did you get them at home? Oh, you have such nice fashion there. I love Gucci. Do you ever wear Gucci? . . . Yeah, it's expensive. . . . You're right. We're all wearing the same thing anymore. It's one world, it's one world. But don't people dress up more there? I have to wear a skirt tonight and I don't want to. Are you an artist? Huh. I thought so. So where are you going next? Tiffany's. Oh, you have to go to Tiffany's. It's right over there, Fifth at Fifty-Seventh. FIFTH AT FIFTY-SEVENTH. You know what? I can show you. Here. I'll get out with you, I was going to get off near here anyway. No, really, it's no bother . . ."

At the southern edge of Central Park, I change buses and we chug onward to the Upper West Side. We go by Lincoln Center, and then I'm back on Broadway, and the scenes unfurl in front of me like ribbons. On the small traffic island on 71st Street between Broadway and Amsterdam, a couple sits eating shish kebabs, tearing off small pieces that they then feed to a little girl in a pink tam who eats a bit, twirls, and then comes back for more. The bus takes a shuddering turn and we rumble past the commercial establishments on 72nd Street — you can get your hair done in cornrows at Afrigenix and then go down a few doors to the Treasures of Judaism. A turn onto Riverside Drive reveals sleds zipping down a hill, the soldier's monument at 90th Street, Grant's Tomb. A shift change at Broadway and 135th, and the bus exhales with impatience, the motor idling while we wait for a new driver.

He takes us further north, to Harlem, to Morningside Heights, and at some point the landscape shift is accompanied by a language change: most of the signs are now in Spanish, advertising the El Mundo department store, the Dentista Hispánico. By 193rd Street, there aren't many people left on the bus, just me and an elderly African-American woman, her hair white wool. She has fallen asleep, and when the bus driver pulls underneath a bridge, announcing that we are at the last stop, her eyes blink open. "I missed my stop!" she says in hurt tones. "I missed my stop!"

The bus driver shakes his mahogany face and smiles at her. "Don't go to sleep on buses, that's what I say," he advises the crestfallen woman as she clambers off the bus.

He turns to me. I know I'm supposed to get off, but I want to make sure that I have gone as far on this island as I can. How much farther is it to the very tip of the island?

"Look over there," the driver says in response, pointing to a thin canal. "Over there, that's the Bronx. You can touch it."

He's not supposed to let me stay on the bus, but he does anyway, saving me a cold wait while he turns the bus around to begin the return portion of his route. I sit as happy as a child because I get to see what happens at the end of the line at the end of the island. He pulls the big beast into the Knightsbridge bus depot and I peer into the large terminal, where empty city buses are parked in no particular order like shucked winter gloves left on the ground.

You might ask why I took this trip, why I took notes on a suitcase soliloquy, why I was so happy to see the inside of a bus terminal. In his essay "Here Is New York," E. B. White contends that there are three New Yorks: one made by the people who were born here; one made by the people who commute here; and one made by what he calls the "settlers," people born elsewhere who move to New York in quest of something. The latter, he writes, embrace the city with the "intense excitement of first love."

Perhaps that is what is happening to me, why I feel this need to travel the length of the island, to have my eyes own what I see, the way you want your hands to own the body of a new lover. I am so content to play this instrument called Manhattan and listen to its music. People in both Minnesota and Manhattan ask me, "Are you a New Yorker now?" and I'm not sure what to say except that I am beginning to find my sense of place here, the same way I did more than a decade ago in another village, one suspended on frozen water.

"No one should come to New York to live," E. B. White says, "unless he is willing to be lucky."

On any random night, I can look out my west windows and see the Hudson. That feels lucky to me. The dark blue of the river takes on a luminescent tone that blends into the coal-colored silhouettes of Hoboken on the other side. The sky is stacked into horizontal stripes of magenta, coral, salmon, the softest yellow, a pale blue, and then the last vestiges of the azure that was there in the afternoon, streaked through with dark gray clouds. A ferry darts across the river, a red light shining at its front. I am surprised how fast it travels.

Hearts

I WAS SOBBING the first time I walked down the aisle. I was five, the flower girl for the nuptials of a second cousin who had been my mother's flower girl, the sort of pretty tradition that is nice to carry on. I wore a little girl's replica of the wedding dress, in matte satin with a lace band at the Empire waist. I also wore a small pillbox hat with a veil. It was 1964, after all.

The tears were prompted by the sudden disappearance of a small strand of pearls I had been given to wear; I was stricken, and within a matter of minutes I had cried myself sick. Matrons hovered around me, alternately shushing my wails and murmuring words of comfort, but I would have none of it. Even then I knew the importance of good accessories. I made it down the aisle, a red-faced and glum little darling, Cupid's pouty emissary. My emotions were writ large on my face: *Forget the ceremony. Where are my pearls?*

We found them later in the day, when I changed clothes after the reception. My mother lifted the satin dress over my curled hair and there the necklace was, nestled neatly into one of the rills of lace on my slip, an undergarment so frilled and tucked that you probably could have secreted an entire jewelry box on its bodice and no one would have known. I had been worrying the clasp before my big walk down the aisle; it must have come undone, the necklace sliding down into its new home. Somewhere, I'm sure, my mother still has that small strand of artificial pearls.

I would walk down the aisle six more times, five of them as a bridesmaid. While many people rue the marriage of Charles and Diana for its headline-inducing glut of misery and marital trauma, I regret it for different reasons. Thanks to her whipped-cream concoction of a wedding dress, I practically drowned in taffeta during my twenties. In one wedding, I was outfitted in a full pink taffeta skirt with pink taffeta rosettes at my waist and breasts, a small pink taffeta-covered hat with feathers bobbing on my head. "You look like a trotter horse," a colleague told me at the reception. Afterward, I burned the headpiece in the parking lot of a 7-Eleven. (An aside to the bride: sorry about that.)

For another ceremony, I wore a more stately lavender number, although the circumference of the sleeves alone would have reduced the wind shear for a small plane and the sash at the back of the dress might have been more appropriate for a royal child's pinafore than for the bustle of a grown woman. Just before the processional, I retired to the lavatory and heard a telltale plopping sound while I sat on the toilet: the ends of the bow had fallen into the bowl. The bride's mother had to wield a blow-dryer to ensure I didn't take those little steps toward the altar with two lengths of wet taffeta slap-slapping my behind.

I still have those dresses in storage somewhere; I always meant to make them into a quilt for a baby's room. Instead, the only time I took them out of storage was for an Ugly Bridesmaid Dress Party. It was an inspired idea: the bouquet-toss competition was the height of the evening. I won a prize that night, a matched set of tacky champagne coupes with BRIDE and GROOM engraved in opaque white letters on the glass. Every one of my dresses was worn by a woman who swore she didn't know what had happened to her own bridesmaid regalia, although after my own incendiary episode with the hat, I had my suspicions.

Three of the five marriages I witnessed in my bridesmaid costumery are still intact, which is better than the national average. One ex-husband picks up his kids at their mother's house with the mistress waiting in the car. Another waited until a week after his daughter's bat mitzvah to decamp his union. The three that survive have their dark moments, I'm sure. Marriage is a mystery, after all. I think of it in terms of the most intimate cartography — an island of two people, shrouded by mist, that those on the shore will never truly be able to see.

At the end of one wedding day, I traipsed upstairs in my taffeta to find the bride sitting on the floor of the carpeted hallway outside her childhood bedroom as the party continued below. You could hear her parents and their friends laughing and the sound of tinkling glass and music. The bride had already changed from white dress to blue jeans. She was smoking, her head tilted up, her eyes slit against the smoke that she exhaled forcibly through her nostrils.

I asked where her husband was, and she nodded toward the bedroom. "He's sleeping it off," she said tightly, and I didn't ask anything more. For some people, "for better or worse" starts early.

They're still married. I am not. A friend recently asked me how I became engaged, and I surprised her by bursting into tears. I used to tell my engagement story because I thought it was funny; then I stopped, all the merriment stripped from the circumstances. As a newlywed, I once attended an all-women brunch. After a few mimosas, the hostess was taken with a fit of boozy candor, telling me with a slight slur, "You just got married because all your friends were getting married." I dismissed her comments at the time, but now I wonder if she wasn't speaking some particle of truth. I don't remember a yearning to ape the actions of others; what I remember from my late twenties was a deep, scraping urge to get on with life. I was tired of floating; I wanted to anchor somewhere. I wanted the rest of my life to begin as soon as possible.

The road to our engagement started with an ultimatum

of sorts. V had been in rehearsals for a new show, and when we returned to my house after the opening-night performance, I sat him down and handed him a brown grocery bag full of the various items he had deposited at my home — a toothbrush, some shirts, a pair of jeans. He could spend the night, I told him, but not in my bed. I had been asking for a commitment for months, and it seemed he couldn't make one.

That was fine, I blithely lied, but I needed to move on. This wasn't an ultimatum, I said, lying again. We were simply through. Then I got up from the sofa and went upstairs to bed, leaving him behind.

He came up to my room three times to tell me how ridiculous I was being. I sent him back down each time.

I cried copiously for three days. And on the third day, he showed up at the door with a limp red rose wrapped in plastic that he had purchased at the Tom Thumb store down the street. It was Easter Sunday. We went to the zoo. As I always told people later, we went and looked at caged animals and decided to get married.

Hilarious so far, isn't it?

I don't remember the actual words of the proposal; what I remember was the deal that followed. We would get married, V said, if I could do one thing: keep my mouth shut. If I could keep our engagement a secret for twenty-four hours, then the deal was on.

I was game, except for the one phone call that by law I thought every woman was entitled to make: I needed to call my mother to tell her the happy news.

No, he said, a deal is a deal.

I offered a counterdeal: two out of three hands of gin rummy. Winner could make the call — or not make it.

I won. Two straight games. We both were stunned at the alacrity with which the cards leaped into my hands. V was barely finished dealing before I slapped my winning hands on the table. I called my mother.

Almost twenty years later, the only thing that makes sense to me about my engagement story is that it ended with a card game. Games of chance were a constant with V and me. We played at least one game of cribbage almost every night that we were married, and the games ended only because the marriage did. It was our way of closing out the day, of catching up with each other. On the nights we were too tired for cribbage, we played gin, our engagement game. It was V who taught me the maxim "lucky in love, unlucky in cards," a line that was used to comfort the loser and tease the winner.

I associate games and cards with some of the happiest hours of my childhood. To this day, I'm attracted to the patterns in games, how a run of numbers seems to stripe a particular hand or a whole evening. For me, opening a hand of cards to see what you have been dealt is akin to sitting in a theater waiting for the curtains to sweep apart. One of my favorite filial memories recalls a family Thanksgiving dominated by a Monopoly game. The men — my grandfather, my father, my uncle — had set the game up on my paternal grandmother's round kitchen table, and my brother and I were allowed to join. Behind us, my mother and both grandmothers did dishes and wrapped leftovers, the clink and thump of china and their fluted murmurs contrasting with the low rumbles of laughter from the game table. My brother was probably only four and close to oblivious of what was happening, but he loved being at the table, his eyes going from one laughing man's face to the next. The joke was that his indifference to the game had somehow led to Monopoly wealth, his pile of play money growing higher and higher. It was cold and gray outside, but we were in warmth, the lamp hanging over the kitchen table tracing a literal family circle, the people I loved either sitting inside its golden light or moving softly around its dark perimeter.

When I married V, I put him in that golden circle.

I got married because that was the template I knew, and I married him because I loved him — his leonine face, the low timbre of his voice, the soft genuine charm that he brought to day-to-day life. We had met dancing, and in the early years of our marriage we still danced. When a show required that he learn how to tango, he would come home and teach me rudimentary steps, and we would dramatically pace up and down the confines of our kitchen to the strains of an Astor Piazzolla album. V is stocky, with a barrel chest, but like many large men, he is surprisingly elegant when he dances.

We were married on a Saturday in May, one week before my thirtieth birthday, in a pavilion on an island in the Mississippi River in downtown Minneapolis. The site was my compromise between his native Paris and my Illinois hometown.

I wore my mother's slipper-satin wedding dress from 1949 and a family ring of diamonds that V's mother had brought from Paris. We had a full moon and a French band with an accordion player, and people still come up to me and tell me what a great time they had that night, the divorce notwithstanding. One of our guests was so ebullient — it might have been the Brouilly — that to our great amusement he came to bid us good luck and good night four times. There is a photograph of me dancing in a ring with the little girls in attendance, none of whom cried because she was missing a strand of pearls. I am laughing, my arms outstretched, and the little girls have shining eyes because they are with the bride.

My wedding album is packed away now in a box, but for years after the divorce it held a designated nook on the bookshelf in my living room, a radioactive little volume that my hand knew to pass when I was searching for the poems and art history sitting nearby. When we get married, we whisper stories to each other: this is how we met, this is how we fell in love, this is what our first kiss was like, this is when I knew. When we get divorced, the stories unravel a bit and we tell them only to ourselves. We have to admit that the old story was more beautiful than what really happened, that maybe we fell in love with our own whispered tales of fidelity and future dances with the same partner, tracing the steps over and over and over again.

Yes, I am still in love with the fairy tale of what I wanted my marriage to be. It's commonplace for cultural critics to wring their hands about the state of marriage, to suggest that if as much thought went into the actual union as went into the ceremony, we would have far fewer divorces. I'm still grateful I had that one day when the dream and the reality were the same. I don't need an album to record the failures of my marriage, but I'm grateful to have a volume that holds the evidence of its days of hope.

People tell you the truth and you don't want to hear it. When we were courting and V told me that he was already married to the theater, I didn't believe him. I was young. By the end of a decade of marriage, I did. Loving him was like loving a caged heart: you might reach out, but your hands touch the bars and nothing else. He was married to his time by himself in the theater's workshop, working on sets; to his time with his colleagues, rehearsing shows; to his time on the stage, when I watched that heart of his take wing. He played Molière's Bourgeois Gentilhomme, he played Jacques Prévert, he played one of Zola's miners; onstage, he had time and tenderness that were his own.

We had been married for a year and a half when the phone rang one morning, early, so that I answered it with surprise. I heard my mother's voice: "Your brother is dead. John's dead." Then I started screaming. I was screaming and on all fours on the bedroom carpet. I was crawling and scratching as if I were on a forest floor, desperate to get away from the bad news and the screams that were coming out of my own mouth. My brother had died the night before and my parents had deemed it too late to call me at midnight; they wanted me to have one last night of normalcy. So they had stayed up, waiting hours with their news before they called.

I have known long-expected deaths after lingering illnesses and I have known sudden deaths. Each has its own kind of pain. My brother had been living with my parents, patching his life back together in the wake of a brutal divorce, attending college classes, working at an electronics retailer, pulling together a band in which he played electric guitar. He had accidentally asphyxiated in his bedroom from a household chemical spray he had been using to clean the strings of that guitar. My father had been retiring for the night, walking slowly down the hall, when he heard my brother's television still droning. He had opened the door to tell my brother to turn off the TV — "It was *David Letterman*," he told me later, even the banal details of the moment fixed for him — and found my brother's body wedged between the wall and the twin bed of his childhood. He had died a week before his twenty-eighth birthday.

I started screaming that morning because of the terrible wrenching grief. Losing a sibling is like losing a limb. Once I received the news that John was dead, part of me was missing. I was screaming in acknowledgment of what was to come, years of phantom pain where my brother should've been attached to me. The only way that V could get me to slow my sobbing and my senseless crawling was to put his whole body on top of me and pin me gently to the carpet, tenderly begging me to stop.

At some point that morning, we were in the bathroom

together. I was sitting on the floor, leaning against the wall, dully watching him shave. I was trying to insert comfort, sense, order on the day. I was making lists, I was stating obvious facts out loud. Of course, I said, you'll be coming to the funeral. V paused before he very carefully reminded me that he had the lead role in his theater's next production, that opening night was only a few days away, that there were no understudies.

I can't recount the exact conversation for you; I can only recount how I remember it, how it became codified in my heart for better and for worse. I remember the feel of the linoleum on my knees because I was kneeling when I begged my husband to come with me to my brother's funeral. He did come — flying in for the day — but I never forgave him for making me beg.

Months later, I was in a car with my best friend from college, the woman who had stood up as our maid of honor. She listened to my recitation of that grief-filled morning and my still acrid anger at V. She took her eyes briefly from the road to lance me with a heartfelt instruction: "You have to get over that." I never did. Instead, I became an angry wife, hoarding the injustices of my marital life, the time V spent away from me, the lack of attention, the silences. I began to envision the theater as a beautiful red-haired woman in a green dress, carefully applying her stage makeup in front of a mirror surrounded with lights. I couldn't compete with the love he had for her, and slowly, bitterly, I began to collect perceived wrongs, amassing them like an old witch stuffing her mouth with dry twigs. It did about as much good.

Once, when we were arguing in our kitchen, I was so angry with V that I took the glass of milk I was holding in my hand and poured it over my head. He stared at me in amazement as the milk dripped from my hair. I had wanted him to see me and to hear me and I couldn't think of any other way to get his attention.

Some of our acquaintances will be surprised at this. "I didn't know it was that bad," they'll say. Maybe they'll remember the party I threw when V turned fifty — the platters of fruit and cheeses and breads, the servers offering red wine and champagne. We gathered around the baby grand piano in the parlor. My voice quavering, I sang, "Another bride, another June / Another sunny honeymoon / Another season, another reason / For making whoopee." It was my favorite silly song, and a circus band had performed it at our wedding reception. A friend turned to me that night, his own marriage in doubt, and said, "I want someone to sing like that to me someday."

I have been thinking about why we get married and why we get divorced, and I wonder if the urge behind both actions is that dissimilar. I wanted to be happy, a desire that strikes me now as a generational marker, a need that is not in the marital lexicon of my parents, who are looking at their fifty-seventh wedding anniversary. It's not that they are unhappy, mind you. I don't think they can envision a life without the other. When my mother started to try to understand why I would leave my marriage, one of her first questions was, "Does he hit you?" Violence is concrete and understandable, but my awkward mucking about for happiness was hard for her to comprehend.

Striving for some kind of happiness in those days, I fell in love with another man, a storyteller. I had a habit, when I was married, of trotting out my collection of stories about being married to a French actor. Since I was so often without him in social settings, I would conjure V up with funny anecdotes, droll self-deprecating set pieces to entertain the people around me. The night I met this man, I was telling him a story that involved one of V's favorite ways to tease me. I would be imitating the people at my office or telling him a story, and he would laugh and shake his head and say, "You are such a shitty actress." He said it with humor and affection, and in his accent it sounded sweet.

But the other man just looked at me and said evenly, "I don't think you're a shitty actress. I think you could do a one-woman show. I'd direct you." He could have touched my face with his hands and it would have had the same effect.

What I remember about those days, my last as a married woman, was the haphazard way I tried to concoct my happiness to make the emotional ends meet. I daydreamed about a triplex where all three of us could live; I woke up in tears from a vision where V was dead and I was free. With a shamed face, I confided that latter dream to a friend who confirmed that she had had her own visions along those lines for her husband. "I always see him getting hit by a car," she said thoughtfully.

When you are about to get divorced, the very molecules

in the air seem to rearrange, unscrambling themselves from the settled life you have known into a new atmosphere full of sharp, flinty edges. Other couples eye you warily and you begin to wonder if you are giving off the stench of failure, like some sort of matrimonial carrion. A friend who had been through her own divorce told me it would be like that for a while: "People are afraid of what you'll show them about their own marriage." I conjured up the image of a marital Diogenes, thrusting his lantern into the caves of other people's unions, exposing whatever was scrawled on the dark walls.

The first time I had to attend a wedding after my divorce, I was saved by a colleague who sat next to me, he in his suit and tie, me in my good wool dress and black picture hat. "I feel like I shouldn't be here," I whispered to him as the organ music wafted through the sacristy and young women in burgundy silk walked down the aisle.

"How do you think I feel?" he whispered back. "I left my wife because I was gay."

When I look out the west windows of my Manhattan apartment, I look almost directly into the windows of an apartment across the way. A couple — a man and a woman — live there, and early in the morning when I am watering the window boxes on my tiny terrace, I can see her on their much larger terrace, inspecting the trees that grow there in tubs. At night, they sit in a ring of light from a table lamp. I am guessing they are in their sixties, and from my observations they appear to be well used to each other's company. I don't mean to stare, and most days I simply catch their movements in my peripheral vision: I'll look up and see one of them crossing the room with a plate or the other reading a newspaper, turning the pages.

I think this is about as close as we ever get to observing anyone else's marriage. My friend John was over not long ago, and I told him that I was worried: the couple across the way was suddenly hugging more often than usual. I was afraid they had received bad news. "Maybe one of them is sick," I said fretfully.

I was standing by the windows, looking into their kitchen. John came to stand beside me and look as well. Suddenly — with a snap we sensed but couldn't hear — the blinds on their windows tumbled down. John and I laughed. We were embarrassed to be caught.

I wonder sometimes what they see when they look over here. Do I seem as though I am well used to my own company? Do I look complete to them? Do they wonder, when they see other people in my apartment, if one of them is a lover? Is it apparent, even across the distance, that I am living a life that I chose?

All through my twenties and thirties I stumbled along looking for happiness. Now I am trying to learn how to be content with the choices I have made. In middle age, we look backward and we look forward. I had time enough to spare, when I was young, to look for happiness. I don't feel that luxury anymore. It has been six years now since the divorce, and it looks to all the world that I have moved on with my life.

People make appreciative noises when they hear that V and I are so amicable, that we visit each other and call in times of need or trouble. My Minnesota bank statement still lists his name after the acronym POD: payment on death, which means that if I die first he will inherit the meager savings still left in that account.

POD was what I feared would happen to me if I didn't make changes in my life; that otherwise, toward its end, I would have to pay for too many paths not taken with wages of regret. So here I am, in a small apartment in Greenwich Village. If I need to look at a picture of marriage, I can look out the window.

Astronauts

When my mother can't sleep, she lies in bed and tries to name the seven original astronauts. During one of my most recent visits home, I ask her during dinner if she can name them. "Alan Shepard, Virgil Grissom, John Glenn, Scott Carpenter," she says, quickly ticking them off, and then she pauses and looks to my father for help.

"Walter Schirra?" he offers, and she nods her assent.

"Walter Schirra," she says firmly, following that up with "and . . . and . . . and . . . Deke Slayton is the seventh one."

"How do you know he's the seventh?" I ask.

"Because he never flew," she says sadly.

"Then who is the sixth?" I ask.

She pauses to think.

"Oh, I can never remember," she says in frustration. After

a moment, she puts down her fork and leaves the dinner table. I can hear her feet hitting the wooden steps to the basement — plonk, plonk, plonk — and then, after a few minutes, I hear the same noise as she makes her way back up — plonk, plonk, plonk. I always have a physical reaction to the sound of my mother's tread in this house, a sort of muscle memory from years of hearing her feet on the floors and steps. The house was built in the early 1970s; the walls are thin, and thanks to the ventilation systems, the sound in one room carries to almost every other room in the house. One afternoon when I was a teenager, I was sitting in the basement, and I thought I would see what it was like to smoke a cigarette. My mother was upstairs in her bedroom. I figured the span of two stories between us made it safe for me to hazard my first smoke, so I opened a window and lit a match. Almost immediately, I heard her feet hit the floor. I knew I was in trouble even when trouble was still two staircases away. As I fumbled to put out the cigarette, I thought to myself, *How does she do that?*

Now my mother returns to the table, brandishing a yellowed newspaper clipping from 1971. And the name of the sixth astronaut is . . .

"Gordon Cooper!" she cries in triumph.

"Does this really help you go to sleep?" I ask.

"No," she says. "Most nights it keeps me up."

I examine the clipping. Attached to it is another yellowed piece of paper, an undated block of newsprint, boxed under the title ASTRONAUT QUIZ. It reads, "Space shots are back in the news . . . best sources say we plan to have an American on the moon before 1970."

"Wow," I say, "you've kept this all this time."

"Oh," she says, "you don't want to know what I have in the basement."

She's right. I don't. Every now and then, when I can't sleep, I think of my parents' basement. When they decided to add a family room on the main floor, they had the contractor dig down there as well. It used to be that after you walked through the TV den set up in the basement, you would enter a room that was neatly divided between the two spheres of the house: my mother's laundry area, with its buckets and bottles and hangers, and my father's workshop, with its old mayonnaise and baby-food jars full of nails and screws. It was sort of like the world of Greek mythology writ small: go to the left and witness the powers of Hera, goddess of domesticity and whiter whites; go to the right and see the awesome might of Zeus's cordless electric drill. Now that room opens up into yet another sphere, a vast underworld of storage space that makes me think of, well, Hades.

Sometimes when I am visiting my parents, they will take me by the hand and lead me to the new storage area. There is so much to see! Furniture is stacked around the perimeter of the room, bureaus and bed stands and frames and chairs from Grandma Lanpher, Grandma Pulliam, Aunt Gertrude, Uncle Bob, my brother, and other offshoots of the family tree. Carefully preserved dresses and school reports reside in coat boxes from stores that went out of business years ago:

Carson Pirie Scott, Peterson's, Archer's. My father is a wood-worker, so the storage room has built-in shelves and lighted closets and handcrafted molding. I can find everything down there, from my old Spirograph drawing kit to gift tags circa 1971 that read FROM SANTA. I know; I've looked.

Whenever we make this little tour, one of my parents will take in the whole room with a glance and say to me, "You'll get it all!" They say it with the sort of cheer you'd hear from a game-show host, but I hear it in the same tone of doom you would expect in a holiday greeting from Tim Burton.

That my mother found that yellowed piece of newsprint about the astronauts isn't very surprising. She is an inveterate clipper of newspaper articles. Most families have one. Every now and then I will receive a bulging envelope with news she thinks I can use: how to get wine stains out of white table-cloths, the history of a Florentine mural, the upcoming one hundredth birthday of a former teacher. I suspect she is still trying to top the piece she clipped years ago from the local crime pages, a multiple-paragraph description of a hapless robber who held up a bank, leaped into his getaway car, led a high-speed chase through a residential neighborhood, lost control of the car, careened through the yards of several houses, and then emerged onto a commercial thoroughfare only to drive the car through the plate-glass window of a storefront.

Why am I reading this? I wondered as I perused sentence after sentence. Then I noticed her neat cursive handwriting running up one margin: "Didn't you go to kindergarten with this man?"

She was right. I had.

We talk nearly every week by phone, usually on Sunday. For a while there, I was getting calls nearly every other day. My father had acquired a cell phone for emergencies when he was in the car. Ever averse to waste, he would call me when he realized he hadn't used all his minutes that month. My mother wouldn't use the cell. She found it distasteful to have to hold such a small thing so close to her head, fearful that it would wreck her weekly wash-and-set. So my father would dial my number to give me the latest on the weather in the Quad Cities or on the tomatoes he was growing at the side of the house.

"Yeah, it's Dad," he'd say when I picked up the phone. "Got some minutes to burn."

For the first year I lived in New York, my mother cried every Sunday when we spoke. "You're just so far away," she would say, her voice quavering, and then she would hand the phone over to my dad. It's probably just as well: sometimes when they try to talk to me at the same time, one of them picking up an extension phone, they have problems hearing each other. Of course, they also have this problem when they are in the same room. My father likes the volume up high on the television in the basement, so loud that the lamps in the living room upstairs begin to vibrate. He swears he does not have a hearing problem; my mother talks too softly, he says. He stops just short of accusing her of doing so on purpose.

My mother — who, it must be admitted, can talk in a whispery rasp sometimes — responds by clipping out a newspaper headline she finds and posting it on the refrigerator. It reads, MY WIFE MUMBLES.

They met on a blind date; they went to the Ice Follies in Rock Island. She was a nursing student in Moline and he was working two jobs, one of them as a grease monkey at an auto shop. One day, a transmission fell on his head; the nurse in the emergency room was dating my father's best friend. She's the one who arranged my parents' first meeting; they have now been married almost fifty-seven years. When I was a little girl, I would beg my mother to get her wedding dress out of the cedar chest where she stored it. Every now and then she would indulge me, holding up the ivory slipper satin, stained with red near the hem where a crepe-paper decoration had bled onto the fabric, probably owing to the snow and slush at their December wedding. I was a child and they were my household gods; seeing the dress was confirmation of the myth that had preceded me.

Years later, when I became engaged to V, they drove up to visit me in St. Paul, taking a room at a discount chain motel. My news had made them nostalgic, and suddenly workaday details came tumbling forth about their own engagement story: how my father had broken up with Mom, saying he needed "more space," how he had changed his mind and gone to see her at the nurse's dormitory, how frustrated he was when he couldn't find her. When he finally did, they went for a short drive, and then he stopped and opened the glove compartment of his car. He handed her a small jewelry box with these stirring words: "Well, did I waste my money?"

I howled when I heard that story, kicking my legs and flopping back on the ribbed cotton bedspread in the motel room. "But that told you everything about the years to come!" I chided my mother, asking incredulously, "That's how he proposed?"

My mother smiled demurely. I turned to my dad. "You needed 'more space'? In 1948?"

He just laughed.

They have made me who I am, these two. What I know about love, how it can be constant, how it can confound, how it sometimes expresses itself in a bickering back-and-forth, I know from them. They have grounded me in the fractious day-to-day of love. These are, after all, two people who celebrated their forty-fifth wedding anniversary by splurging on an imported porcelain toilet for the downstairs bathroom. Now, at seventy-seven, they hide Christmas gifts from each other around the house.

When I was still living in Minnesota, during a visit to my parents' in Illinois, I confessed to my mother — shakily, as if it were an intimate, great secret — that I wanted to write fiction. Somewhere inside of me, I was sure, was a novelist. She nodded her head and sniffed.

"Well," she said, "your best material is three hundred miles away."

She was right. Only now that I live in New York, my best material is eight hundred miles away.

When I want a portrait of parental love, I think of the first night I had my official driver's license. I had begged to borrow my dad's car, a bottle-green Maverick that he used to drive to work, our family's first second car. Permission attained, I loaded it up with my three best friends and we went cruising up and down the main drag of our hometown, past strip malls and burger joints, and then through the different neighborhoods where the cool boys lived. We had our own version of Dead Man's Hill, and the first time I took it fast, we hit the bottom of the slope and the car popped up into the air. Our heads hit the roof. We laughed and laughed. So I did it again and then again, filling the compact with our squeals and screams.

And then I went too fast and hit a curve. The wheels struck the raised curb, propelling the car off the road and into a small patch of woods. I didn't even try to steer, which was probably a blessing, the car shooting past two trees so close that they sheared off the side-view mirrors on both sides. We landed with a thump and at a near right angle to the ground, at the bottom of a ravine. We could hear the sirens even before we climbed out of the car, shocked and quiet, slipping on the leaves on our way back up to the road.

The clearest memory I have of that night is not of the accident itself or of squad cars with their accusing red lights or of the ambulance that, thank God, we didn't need. It's not of the first sight I had of my parents, their faces drawn as they got out of our other car, the sensible sedan. It's of later that night, after we all finally went home, when I was walking to my bedroom, past the room my parents shared. My father was standing at his desk, his arms on a chair for support. I was used to the sight of him sitting in that chair: that's where he paid the bills, carefully writing out the checks. He was standing with his back to me, and the slope of his shoulders was eloquent. They were bowed in grief, and I think he was, ever so slightly, shaking.

This is how young I was: I thought he was sad about the damaged car.

I was in my first year or so of college, telling the story about that night to some friends, when that image of my father flashed in front of me and I suddenly realized that he had been standing there in a mixture of agony and relief — agony at getting the phone call where someone says "Your daughter has been in an accident" and relief that I had survived it.

Sometimes I think it is amazing that my parents survived the raising of me.

My mother and I used to vex each other. I can remember standing in front of her with a packed suitcase, intent on running away. I was six and holding a doll-size piece of luggage packed with washcloths, an angry little girl who finally consented to stay. By the time I entered my teens, our arguments had heat to them, mother-daughter shopping trips that ended with the two of us sitting stone-faced during the car ride home and me slamming doors once we arrived there. We argued over the clothes I wore, the food I ate or didn't eat, how much time I spent with my friends. I felt the injustice of it all very keenly, and detailed my complaints to my friends as we walked back and forth to school. When I was a young adult, I ran into a playmate from junior high. She had been a little wren of a thing, with lank white-blond hair and blue cat's-eye glasses. Now she stood before me, newly attractive in her contact lenses, her hair in an attractive gamine cut. And here is what she wanted to know: Did I still hate my mother? I just stared at her, trying to think how she could remember me that way.

My mother is reticent to part with details about her childhood, but I have seen just enough to conjecture that she knew few comforts. She was the only child of a gentleman farmer and his second wife; her only sibling was a much older half brother. Her father died when she was eleven and her circumstances changed drastically. She and her mother soon moved from the farm to a tiny frame house in a small farming community in Mercer County, Illinois, where they were, as far as I can tell, genteelly poor. It's not that she wanted so badly to become a nurse, she told me once; it was that she had so few choices, because of her gender and her class and the times in which she lived.

She and my father raised me with an implied pattern and promise of improvement: I would be the first in either of their families to go to college, I would make a better living than those who went before me. At the same time, I felt an implied pattern and promise of attachment: don't do too well, don't go too far away. I confounded them with my desires and ambitions. I can tell you that we were on 23rd Avenue in Moline and had just passed 16th Street when I looked out the window of the family sedan one afternoon and airily announced to my father, the sole other occupant of the car, that I wasn't going to stay in town once I graduated from high school. I was twelve. I felt it was incumbent upon me to let him know my intentions, I am guessing more for my sake than for his. I don't remember his response. During my senior year of college, I was awarded an internship at a Detroit newspaper. My father couldn't understand how the offer was remotely attractive, given that he could arrange a summer job that would allow me to live at home and save money. "It would be good for my career," I told him. "It would make me happy." It was the "happy" part that stumped him. My mother, whenever I would unfold my latest plans and ambitions, would merely sigh. "You always shoot for the moon," she would say with worry.

I think that was the source of much of our friction when I was growing up. She was giving me the childhood she never had: I was cosseted and loved, read to from the classics during lunch, given as much advantage as she and my father could offer. But there was a push-pull to the arrangement that she hadn't bargained for: what happens if you build a bridge for your children and they actually cross it? The toll it exacts might be unexpected for both parent and child. The only way my family could afford to send me to the college I wished to attend was for my mother to go back to school, relearn a new nursing curriculum, and then return to work after fifteen years as a stay-at-home mom. She came home from night classes with heavy medical textbooks, doing her homework in addition to her housework. When she found a job, it was at a nursing home, where she was known for the tenderness of her care and the way she protected her charges.

I had difficulty adjusting to college, and I called home one night, depressed, mewling that my classes were harder than I thought they would be, that I felt lonely, that I wasn't sure about my major.

"What's wrong?" my exhausted mother asked tartly. "Cheese slip off the cracker?"

That brought me back to my senses in a hurry.

For much of my life, I have felt as if I were straddling two worlds: the one I came from, with coffee at supper and grace before meals and the Nicene Creed recited on Communion Sunday mornings in a blond-wood church; and the one I live in now, which is none of those things.

I was at a reading and literary discussion on the Upper East Side one night, a gathering of stock characters that resembled an early Woody Allen movie. Men sporting tweed jackets and goatees sat next to women wearing heavy sculptural jewelry and indigenous fabrics. One woman's head was shaved, probably as a protest against the hegemony of hair. It was that kind of crowd. My fingers itched to do something, anything, to puncture the pretension. I started to think about Grandma Lanpher, who said "hamburg" instead of "hamburger" and who served us a ketchup-encrusted meat loaf almost every Wednesday evening of my childhood. I wondered what she would make of the company her granddaughter was keeping right now.

During the question-and-answer period of the evening, a woman not far from me stood up, flicked her long, burnt-velvet scarf over her shoulder, and introduced herself to the room by saying that she wrote film reviews for a psycho-analytic journal, adding that what she had heard so far this evening was reifying the distinction for her between imagination and memory. I think it was on the third use of the word "reify" when I began to twitch seriously, seized with an almost unbearable urge to stand up and shout, "Who wants a meat loaf sandwich?" I guess you could say that moment reified my affection for my upbringing, despite the distance I had traveled to supersede it.

I think back to that moment when I stood in front of my mother with my toy suitcase full of washcloths. When I told that story recently to a friend, she laughed and recalled her own childish attempts at running away. "My mother always let me go," she told me. "She knew eventually I would get hungry and come back." My mother pleaded with me to stay.

It was only years later that I thought the episode might have had a different resonance for her because I was adopted, picked up when I was six weeks old from a Lutheran social-services agency in Chicago. My parents had been married for a decade, and they placed me in the backseat of the car in a traveling crib, their necks constantly craning to look at me as they drove the four hours across the state back to the town on the Mississippi River where they would raise me. It's a wonder, my mother said when she first recounted that story, that they didn't get in a wreck.

My brother and I were both adopted and had different birth mothers. Inevitably, if the subject of adoption comes up in a conversation, the first thing people ask is, "Do you know your real mother?" And then I have to give them a gentle corrective: it's *birth* mother. Of course there's a story there, a story of a woman courageous enough to give up her child, a story of her own loss and how she bore it after bearing a child. It's just that, as I get older, it's the story of my parents, the people who raised me, that I wish people would ask me about instead. That is the story I can't seem to get enough of now.

The last time I was home, my mother and I were doing dishes, replicating a stance from my childhood, her hands in the sink, me standing to the right with a dish towel. She lifted her hands from the water to show me the ravages of her arthritis, the joints of her fingers in painful crooks, the bones in wayward zigs and zags. The pads of flesh on her fingertips were riven with tiny cuts. "It's the pressure," she said. "Whenever I do anything, the skin just cuts open."

I took her hands in mine. At moments like this, I want to gather her in my arms, as if she were a bird, and feel her wings flutter against my embrace. Do I know my real mother? Yes, I do. She lies in bed at night, her white hair against the pillow, and tries to name the original astronauts. They began their mission the year I was born. In my mind's eye, my mother lies in bed and stares at the ceiling. She remembers that Deke Slayton didn't get to fly but that her daughter did.

Heaven

THIS IS WHAT HEAVEN LOOKS LIKE: You are surrounded by beauty. When you look up, you see puffy clouds tinged with rose and coral. You're not alone but you're still by yourself. You are perfectly content. It's Heaven, after all, so you can have practically any book you want. And laptops are banned from the last three reading tables.

The main reading room at the New York Public Library is my version of a holy place. I sit in the back of the south end, so the room stretches in front of me, rows upon rows of tables with shaded lamps, three-tiered chandeliers dropping down from the ceiling, color blocks of reference books lining the walls. In the middle of this grand salon of literature is an arched wooden divider that lends the room an ecclesiastical air, heightened by the ornate moldings on the ceiling, which surround the murals of those pastel-touched clouds.

People sit in pewlike benches near the front of the room, looking at a digital screen that displays the numbers assigned to book requests. They study the screen with such purposeful intensity that they could be looking at a train schedule, waiting for the express, or waiting, perhaps, for their celestial assignment.

From my perch in the back, I observe the people around me. The woman next to me is diligently copying sentences from *Adams vs. Jefferson: The Tumultuous Election of 1800.* At the table across from mine, a woman is holding a sheaf of handwritten pages, her mouth held in a wide stretch as she reads. A few tables up, a clutch of schoolboys in navy blazers whisper fiercely to one another and clap their hands over their mouths to muffle laughter. A man with his hair in short dreadlocks shuffles around, a turquoise-and-blue blanket underneath his backpack. His face is slightly confused, you get the feeling that he is living on a slightly different planet from the one the rest of us wake up to — yet he alarms no one. People see him and study him for a minute and then let him be.

That, I decide, is the music of this room — the sound of letting things be. You hear the occasional scrape of a chair, the paper-on-paper slide of turning pages, the small metallic clicks produced by fingers on keyboards. Pens scratch on paper, books thump into return bins. When people talk, it is sotto voce, the way you would in a house of worship.

Reading is akin to worship, an intensely private act of focused meditation that can be achieved in a communal setting. These days, sitting in a library and reading is the closest I get to flirting with the eternal questions and verities, although I talk to God all the time, in conversations that range from panicky entreaties of "ohpleaseohpleaseohplease" to whispers of gratitude for more peaceful moments such as, say, walking along the Hudson. I talk to God even though I'm not sure God exists: one of us has a commitment problem.

I was raised in the Lutheran Church — Missouri Synod (if the title confuses you, don't worry; I didn't know what a "synod" was for years myself) and confirmed by a pastor named Eldor Haake. He was a man of staunch faith; all you had to do was look at him to know it. With his silver-and-black hair, dark brows, and grim visage, and with his pastoral robes, he was, literally, a man of black and white. Either you were saved by the one true church or you were damned. Women were subservient to men; homosexuality was a sin. When I was a teenager, a visiting vicar climbed up to the pulpit one day and began his sermon with a joke — a joke! — which right there put him out as different. The joke went like this: A man dies and goes to Heaven, where St. Peter is giving him a tour. He notices a large red-velvet curtain that hangs over one section of Heaven, obscuring it from the rest. "What's that for?" he asks. "Shhhh," the angel replies, "that's for the Missouri Synod Lutherans. They think they're the only ones up here."

That vicar didn't last long, as I recall.

As a child, my spiritual questing was mostly limited to moments of stark terror: I was afraid I would go to Hell. When I was six, my father refashioned the attic of our little starter house into a bedroom, with sloping walls and dormers covered in wood paneling. I was given a big bed, and my mother would climb the narrow stairs to the attic each night to tuck me in and solemnly oversee the simple prayer I had been taught to recite: "Now I lay me down to sleep, I pray the Lord my soul to keep. If I should die before I wake, I pray the Lord my soul to take. Amen." Some nights, the starch and sobriety of that last couplet alone were enough to keep me from sleep. Apparently, there was a chance I might die before I woke up — and the best we could do was to beg God to take me in.

When I looked up from my bed at the paneling overhead, the grain in the wood would slowly dissolve into the distorted faces of monsters, their mouths curled in screams. I could hear the faint swish of automotive traffic outside my window; car headlights would intersect with streetlamps to create long sinuous shadows that moved along my bed at a menacing pace. I thought they were thick black snakes crawling up the covers. Since my imagination gave equal time to the devil, I also worried about vampires and werewolves and so kept the sheets pulled tight around my neck.

I would pray, but when things got really bad, I would also call out for my mother, in a thin and reedy voice that compassed the long distance between my room and that of my parents downstairs. While I waited for rescue, I would think about the stories we had heard at Sunday school: Daniel in the lion's den, Jonah in the belly of the whale, the three Christian servants thrown into the furnace to prove their faith. And then, of course, there was the crucifixion. When you are afraid that you might die before you wake because of vampires or wood-paneling monsters, just picturing Jesus on the cross concentrates the mind in a powerful way.

As I got older, I started to ask questions. The gender roles at church especially bothered me. Why were only men pastors? And ushers? And those passing out the plate at offertory? Why were only boys allowed to be acolytes, lighting the candles and then sitting in the front pew? Why did God want men to collect the money and then women to gather and count it later in the church office? Where was it written in holy scripture that women served Jesus by wearing aprons and doling out food from Tupperware containers in the church basement? It didn't make sense.

And then feminism came to Holy Cross Missouri Synod Lutheran Church, or, at least, my version of feminism. A young-adult service was inaugurated for the teens. While the smaller children were in their Sunday school classes, we would gather in the sanctuary and partake in our own miniversion of an adult service. I think it was a way to acknowledge that we had moved beyond the Old Testament coloring books and were ready to grapple with the bigger questions. Those of us in the seventh and eighth grades were enrolled in confirmation classes, long and tedious hours of instruction that hovered over Saturday mornings like gray clouds.

Confirmation class did at least bring a sort of democratic spirit back to adolescence. All the social barriers that functioned at junior high school — the divisions between jocks and hoods, cheerleaders and geeks — were erased by the united desire of our parents that we be confirmed. So I would sit across from Teena Blackstok, who would barely speak to me at Wilson Junior High, and sneak glances at a boy named Neil from a rival school who wore a black leather jacket and had greasy hair and thus seemed vaguely dangerous. None of us wanted to be there, and even now I feel sorry for the poor red-haired vicar who was assigned to our class, a man with a terrible overbite and watery eyes.

It was the director of children's education who gave in to my pleas to be the first female acolyte at Holy Cross. OK, so it wasn't one of the real services, just our truncated young-adult ritual, but it was a start, wasn't it? I roped in Renee Wegeman to do the honors with me; we had known each other since Vacation Bible School days. Walking down the aisle, I could feel my hands shaking. The sanctuary sure looked different when you were part of the service as opposed to sitting as a supplicant in a pew. We were handed long brass lances that had both a wick and a small bell-shaped snuffer at the far end. You lit the wick at the beginning of the service so you could light the candles on the altar; at the end of the service, you snuffed out the candles with the little bell. Renee and I lit the candles and then went to sit in the first pew, right beside the aisle, in the space traditionally reserved for the acolytes.

Behind us sat a group of boys who, up until now, had always performed that service. They were older, maybe fifteen or sixteen, and they didn't like what we were up to.

"Stupid," one of them hissed as we sat down.

"Stupid, stupid, stupid" came the refrain from the others.

Their whispered catcalls didn't let up. Renee looked at me with annoyance. What had I gotten her into? The critique continued: we were dumb, we were stupid, we were girls. The director of children's education was giving the sermon that day — I could not tell you the first thing he said — and as he was finishing up, one of the boys leaned over into our pew and whispered with real urgency, "Go! Go! Go! You're supposed to put out the candles now!"

I looked at Renee and pulled her hand. *We'll show them*, I thought. She resisted. The commands from the pew behind us grew in intensity. "Losers. You're supposed to go up now!"

I pulled at Renee again and we stood up, walking into the main aisle of the church. With great solemnity, we picked up the brass candlelighters, walked in a pious cadence to the altar, and capped each flame with the brass hood. Thin little trails of white smoke went up into the air. As we walked down the altar steps and passed the director of children's education, I noticed a puzzled look on his face. Then my eyes went to the boys in the second pew, all of them laughing now, their mouths open as they slapped hands in high fives. We had gone up too early; the service was only half-over.

Do you remember how in adolescence even the color of your shoes was something that could bring on a fit of agony?

How your mother calling you back to the car in front of the school because you had forgotten something could make you flush in shame? We had screwed up for Jesus in front of a large group of our peers. Renee glowered at me with something akin to hate in her eyes. In my mind's eye, we just kept walking, down the aisle, past the other pews, and out of the sanctuary, a sanctuary no more for the likes of us.

Contrary to what you might think, that episode didn't destroy my faith. I was duly confirmed, although I spent the night before my confirmation reading Lloyd C. Douglas's novel *The Robe,* because it satisfied my need to attach some passion to the event. I was lacking real conviction for the ceremony, and it bothered me. I was a dutiful daughter and wanted to be of the spirit. Before I left for college, I even asked Pastor Haake for the addresses of some Missouri Synod churches in Chicago. "He was so happy you did that," my mother reported later.

It would have given him pain then to see how easily I slipped the straitlaced bonds of his church. I had brought my Luther's Catechism along with me to college and placed it into my bookcase. My friend Mark found it there — my wonderful, gay, Jewish friend Mark. He looked up in alarm when I walked into my dorm room and found him sitting at my desk, reading the rules of my church. He was appalled.

"Do you really think I'm going to Hell just because I'm Jewish?" he asked. "That makes no sense. Do you really believe that? Tell me you don't believe it." I didn't. And in that one little moment, I left the church.

I believe that departure caused my parents pain, although we rarely talk about it. In the last few years that I lived in St. Paul, I would attend Christmas and Easter services at an Episcopal church down the street. Yes, yes, I know — the worst kind of Christian, the kind who turns up only for the big days. I don't claim to be observant; for me, going to those holy-day services was like touching the hem of a sacred raiment. I used to know what it felt like and I wanted to reassure myself that the fabric was still there. My father remains a church elder in Moline; for several years there, my mother was an avid student of the scripture lessons conducted by Pastor Haake's successor, sessions in which they made serious studies of the texts. In the wake of 9/11, the church group even took up a study of Islam.

"We are all the children of Abraham," my mother informed me one Sunday on the phone.

When my brother died, Pastor Haake was still at the helm of Holy Cross, and he conducted the service in one of the main rooms of a family-run funeral home in downtown Moline. Let's call it Brownbeck's. In the days following my brother's death, the earth was a flattened, windswept landscape. I felt as if my veins had turned to glass, like hollow tubes; instead of blood coursing through me, air whistled through my body, making a sound that only I could hear. I caromed from extreme to extreme, from ground-hugging despair to giddy heights of hilarity. We were ushered tactfully into a room where models of caskets stood on display. It looked like a car dealer's showroom, and I am here to tell you that there really is nothing like that new casket smell. Standing over a coffin lined with an incongruously cheery orange silk, my parents and I talked about which clothes my brother should wear to his own funeral. I made an argument for his cowboy boots. "That way we can say he died with his boots on," I suggested helpfully. I discovered it is possible to be in the middle of howling grief and still find room to despair of the mortuary's flocked wallpaper. Some days, the only way I could function was to turn myself into a reporter and start totting up the details around me: the folding chairs lined up for the service, the wood paneling on the wall, the lemon yellow paint in the hallway.

My brother, John, had worked at a big-box electronics store, and his coworkers came to the service, their faces riven in shock that someone their age could die. Pastor Haake stood in front of the assembled mourners and had just begun speaking when there was a commotion in the back, a noise that sounded like the squeal of a pig. It was, in fact, a pig: a Vietnamese potbellied pig trotting down the aisle toward the casket. A funeral-home employee, a large blond woman who resembled Joan Blondell, was leaning against a doorway, shaking her head. "There goes Grover," she said dryly.

Grover belonged to Mr. Brownbeck. Having made too many messes at the Brownbeck family home, Grover had been banished to the mortuary, where he was supposed to stay put in Mr. Brownbeck's office, a repository of all things porcine — mugs, pencils, prints, and magnets. Somehow, Grover had managed to slip out the door.

Every funeral needs a pig. I hope there's one at mine. Pigs don't mind the dead and they cheer up the living. I watched my father, his face a ravaged shell, laugh despite himself. It was a respite, if only for a moment, as if a pair of hands had tilted his face upward, smoothed his forehead, touched his cheeks so they lifted in a smile.

Even Pastor Haake laughed.

My brother died a week before his twenty-eighth birthday, and I stayed with my parents until his birthday passed. The morning he would have turned twenty-eight, I was still in bed when I heard an awful sound come from my parents' room. It was my mother, keening, a long and sustained note of loss, as if she had opened her mouth to breathe and a terrible groan had barreled out of her instead. I understood then why some people throw themselves into graves or hold on to caskets and won't let go. When she was done, a silence descended on the house, and it was even worse than the keening.

It was around that time that I began making my peace with organized religion, specifically the one in which I had been raised. Some knot of anger in me began to work itself loose. There are plenty of things I don't like about that church, and, sure, whenever I attend services I'm tempted to fill out the little comment cards they leave in the pews next to the offertory envelopes: "Martin Luther would have ordained a woman by now." But I don't. I have seen this church give sustenance to good people, and at some point that became enough for me. We're all the children of Abraham, after all.

But leaving one church doesn't predicate that you go on to another one, and I have handled my spiritual life in much the same way that other people deal with sex or money: I just don't talk about it. Given that I was raised with such stern admonitions about the ever-looming threat of Hell, it seems funny to me now that I could walk away so easily from those precepts, leaving them behind like a suit of clothes left rumpled on the floor. I was a college student paying a social call to the mother of a high school friend when the subject of religion came up, and I began to explicate how I thought that there was probably a Great Consciousness or some sort of creative power, but that I wasn't sure there was a God. "Oh, Kathy," the mother said firmly, batting away my half-formed assertions as if they were flies, "you don't believe that." Not only was she firm in her faith — she was a practicing Catholic — but she was firm in my faith as well. It was inconceivable to her that I could question the existence of God.

Here's what I don't question: faith itself. The older I get, the more beautiful it appears to me, even if I remain mystified by how one attains it. Former poet laureate Robert Pinsky says that the medium for poetry is the breath of each reader, the voice — both internal and heard — that sounds out the syllables that make up a line or a stanza. The medium for faith, I think, is will.

If I have faith in anything, it's in books, in the written human record, in the old, old miracle of one sentence strung to another and yet another. I sit at the polished oak table in the Rose Reading Room at the New York Public Library. When I look up from my book, I realize that the identities and con-figurations of the people around me have shifted. The boys in the blazers have gone, the woman next to me has slipped away. I have been so absorbed that I haven't noticed. It's as if I had blinked and they had vanished. We're here for such a short while. But that's how it is, here in Heaven and on Earth.

That Girl

LET ME TELL YOU how I became a feminist. It was easy. On Friday afternoons, the two sixth-grade classes at Franklin Elementary School would gather in Mr. Rogiers's room for a debate on current events. He would announce the topic — Should there be a death penalty? Should we pull out of Vietnam? — and then we would scamper to whichever side of the room had been labeled PRO or CON, depending on our point of view. One day, the topic was the Women's Liberation Movement. Or, as the activists in the movement were called back then, the "women's libbers."

I ran to the PRO side, afraid that in the crush I might get pushed to the back. Imagine my surprise when I skidded to a stop, looked around, and realized that I was the lone advocate for feminism. In a moment of chivalry, Mr. Rogiers walked over to my side of the room so that I would have some company.

I don't remember much about that debate, just that the real arguments were presented afterward on the playground, where they always were. It was hard to argue concepts such as equality and discrimination when what most of the boys and girls wanted to know was whether I was going to burn my bra. Since this was the sixth grade, just the mention of a bra induced embarrassment. It had been only a matter of months since the purchase of this item at the mod and oh-so-swinging Juniors Department of the Peterson Harned Von Maur department store in Davenport. The image still loomed in my head of the scary, large-bosomed woman with the tape measure who had fitted me.

I was marked for the rest of my grade-school career as the bra-burning women's libber. When the end of the year rolled around, I was one of the students asked to compose prophecies for those of us graduating on to seventh grade and junior high, so I was standing in front of the assembly of parents and students when my own fortune was read, one not of my authorship: I would take over a men's underwear company and become its president. Hey, sixth-grade humor is like that. The people in the audience laughed and laughed. My parents were there. They were laughing too. I turned bright red.

My girlhood encompassed Barbie and Betty Friedan's *The Feminine Mystique,* Archie comics and Marlo Thomas in *That Girl,* old Doris Day movies and Gloria Steinem. It was all one world to me, seamless. I would crib my mother's issues of *McCall's* magazine and read Betty's columns every month, and then I would climb the stairs to my attic bedroom and set up my doll furniture on my mother's old desk with the flip-down shelf. It made the perfect studio apartment.

My Barbie had countless weddings, played Cinderella, and presided over King Arthur's Court, but she also flew off on job interviews. Unprompted by anything I observed in the lives around me, my idea of adulthood was to dress in a red suit, wear a big picture hat, and jet to New York. So that's what my Barbie did. The destination was thanks to Marlo Thomas, who played Ann Marie in *That Girl,* one of the first TV sitcoms to portray what was then sweetly known as a "career woman." I didn't know that; I just knew that, along with prom dresses and bridal gowns, my Barbie also came with luggage and a convertible. She could go places, and so, vicariously, could I.

Years later, I'm at a United Nations reception in New York for the first international conference on girls' rights. I'm there as a reporter covering the young female delegates from Minnesota who are attending. The topics at hand are serious: How do we prevent gender discrimination, which in some cultures starts when the girl-child is in the womb? How do we ensure that girls get an education? That they are safe from abuse and human trafficking? I'm also making repeated phone calls to an assistant for Kofi Annan, who is rumored to be named the next secretary-general and who has an unlikely connection to Minnesota — he went to Macalester College in St. Paul. "I think we might be able to arrange an interview," the assistant says, and I call my editor with the good news.

Then Marlo Thomas walks in the room and suddenly I am six years old, glued to a black-and-white TV. I can still hum the theme song to *That Girl,* and while one part of my brain is absorbing the statistics about girls and education, the other part is lustily singing the words to the theme song: "Diamonds, Daisies, Snowflakes . . . That Girl!" I can assure you this wouldn't be happening if I were talking to Kofi Annan. I approach Marlo. She probably wants to talk about the Girls' Bill of Rights or the horror of prenatal sex selection. I want to tell her how *That Girl* changed my life, and those are the words coming out of my mouth. She smiles and nods, but halfway through my comments — maybe when I introduce the Barbie part of the story — her eyes begin to glaze over in a look that says, "Get security."

I excuse myself and return to interviewing pint-size feminists who probably would hoot at *That Girl;* to them, Marlo Thomas is the woman from *Free to Be . . . You and Me,* a woman who helped shape the way they see the world and their place in it. She did the same thing for me, of course, just in a different era, in a different form.

As a little girl, I presided over a vast Barbie queendom, populated by such Barbie associates as Francie, the teen with the groovy blond hair; Skipper, the little sister; and Stacey, the talking doll with a British accent. To this day, my mother rues our acquisition of Stacey; she was free with the trade-in of my original Barbie with the brunette ponytail. It was a rash move. Every now and then, when the subject of my childhood toys comes up, my mother gets a faraway look in her eyes and I know she is thinking of the school loans I could have paid off had we only held on to my vintage Barbie until I was vintage myself.

At least we still have Midge.

Midge was Barbie's best friend, the not-quite-as-pretty, perky one. You knew that because she had brown hair in a flip and freckles dusting her nose. If Barbie was Miss America, Midge was Miss Congeniality, the person whom Barbie called to do something with if Ken was busy. It was Barbie who got to wear "Solo in the Spotlight," the strapless black sheath appropriate for singing torch-song standards at a night-club; Midge was happier in gingham. As a child, I was a keen observer of the genus *Barbie*, and I knew, even then, that Midge's very existence was telling me something important: we don't all get to be Barbies. As a little girl with brown hair and freckles, I foresaw a Midge-like future ahead of me.

The world was bristling with such messages. I knew from reading Archie comics that there were two main female archetypes in high school: Betty and Veronica. Betty was the dependable, friendly, middle-class blonde; Veronica was the spoiled, sable-haired beauty whom all the boys tried to impress. You were either a Betty or a Veronica in life, and it seemed best to make your peace early on with what fate had handed you. Just as I recognized myself in Midge, I knew that I ended up on the Betty end of the spectrum.

Barbie and I were born the same year, and occasionally I like to compare our progress. She has kept her figure, but I've amassed a life. It amuses me to think of a middle-aged Barbie and what she might look like — somehow I imagine that she would still be thin. Why, I wonder, has Midge gone off into obscurity, known and remembered only by little girls born in the late 1950s? Midge must have actually aged, her plastic waist thickening, her arched, knobby breasts softer now and resting lower on her plastic molded trunk. Barbie never had the mess of a menstrual cycle, but I imagine Midge is going to have a lot to say about menopause.

The last time I played with a Barbie doll, I was in Kathy Anderson's darkened bedroom, the two of us furtively selecting Barbie outfits, the shades pulled down so that the kids outside couldn't see what we were doing. We were in the sixth grade, too old for dolls, already eyeing the bubblegum-pink Yardley Lip Slickers in the makeup aisle at the drugstore. We were also already slowly growing apart, the cruel clock of adolescence pushing us into different development time zones. Kathy had long blond hair, baby blue eyes, and breasts: she didn't need a teen Barbie; she was a teen Barbie. Kathy would be using the Lip Slickers long before I would. One of the last times I was at her house — not much different from my own — I asked her father why Kathy was on a diet. It didn't make sense to me. He was a workingman, eating an early dinner at his kitchen table when I posed the question, and he didn't look up as he replied, "If she doesn't watch her figure, no one else will."

But that afternoon in her bedroom, our concerns were narrowed to the whoops and hollers of the kids outside, intruding on our serious, secret play. There was something shameful to what we were doing, as if we were going against the tides of nature; we played halfheartedly and soon quit. After that, I never picked up a doll again unless it was as an act of nostalgia. I was twelve going on thirteen, and my play days were over.

Because of her place in my childhood, I have a soft spot for Barbie, even as a feminist. Or perhaps I should amend that to: especially as a feminist. What I remember most about my games with her was the sense of limitless possibilities, the memories of which I clung to when I began to encounter the real world.

It was only a year or so after that sixth-grade debate when I was with my family at one of our favorite ice-cream shops, a little store tucked away in a strip mall not far from our house. The family joke was that, despite the vast array of flavors, my brother always ordered vanilla. I, on the other hand, would pace the length of the coolers, looking down at all the different options, drawing out the delicious anticipation. Did I feel like German chocolate cake? Or mint chocolate chip? I loved that store and I couldn't imagine a better job than to be behind the counter, scooping that beautiful ice cream. I went over to my dad and told him I'd like to work there someday. "Go ahead." He motioned with his cone to the owner, a genial white-haired man who greeted us with a big smile whenever we came in. "Go and tell him."

So I did. I walked over and told him that in a year or so I would be able to get a work permit and that I loved his store and that I wanted to work there someday. And Mr. Genial looked down at me, a little junior high girl with long hair and barrettes and freckles, and said, "I'm sorry, honey. I don't hire girls."

I remain a little chagrined that my big moment of radicalization happened over a tub of fudge nut swirl. Still, something elemental in me sharpened, took note of the world around me in a way it hadn't before. I couldn't scoop ice cream? Because I was a girl? His policy made no sense. As the shock faded, the injustice of it made me seethe.

To this day, when I walk in a newsroom or an office or read a contributors' list in a magazine, my eyes do an almost involuntary sweep, a sort of Geiger gender counter, to see if women are represented. I'm not ashamed of that; I'm just sorry that it still feels necessary to count. When I was a newspaper columnist, a supportive editor wrote to a contact she had at a syndication service; she thought my column was good enough to run in other papers. But her contact wrote back that most papers already had a woman or two on the editorial page; any more would be redundant.

I hope I don't have to spell that one out for you. But trust me, it's about as dumb as saying someone with ovaries can't scoop ice cream. If having more than one or two women on an editorial page is redundant, then what is having more than two men?

When I became a columnist, I was the first woman at the *St. Paul Pioneer Press* to have a designated space on page one of the metro news section, the same as the male columnists. The job had been posted for a woman. I was standing in front of the newsroom bulletin board, reading the job description, when an affable sportswriter, a man I'd always liked, walked over to me and said, "Wish I was a woman so I could get a column."

Without thinking, I said, "Yeah, well, if I were a man, I'd already have one." He walked away.

In one of my early columns, I made fun of the Clinton administration for its "don't ask, don't tell" policy on gay soldiers. I recommended that if assembling a top-notch heterosexual fighting force was such a priority, perhaps the government should look to people who knew about the hard combat of survival and gutting it out: they could draft single mothers. My husband was on tour the week that column ran, and I was alone in the house, putting away groceries, when I stopped for a moment and pushed the button on the answering machine. I had my hand on a can of tuna when I heard "Read your column. You smart-ass cynical bitch. Guess who dies next?"

I had received various threatening and demeaning letters and calls in my career and usually just shrugged them off, but something in the tone of the caller's voice sounded purposeful. Like he meant it. I spent the night at a friend's house and the next day met a locksmith whom I had called to install security latches on the ground-floor windows.

He had a kind and creased face, and he meant well when he looked at me while he was figuring out his bill and said, "Maybe you ought to write about things that are less controversial — you know, like motherhood."

I smiled, but what I really wanted to do was grab him by the collar and shout, "Write about motherhood? Do you want to get me shot?"

Maybe motherhood wasn't controversial to him, but in my circles it sure was. Do you have a kid or decide not to have one? Do you stay home with the kid or not? Do you sacrifice a career for the kid or not? Do you try to have it all? Is it even remotely possible to make any of these choices and then not to judge other women when they arrive at different conclusions?

Of course, questions like that were why I had a column, why I had been given a public voice. What still strikes me as odd, though, is that it was such a new idea in the final decade of the twentieth century that I would be appointed the first female news columnist in St. Paul and that someone's reaction after reading my column was to phone my home and threaten me.

The first phone call I made after I heard that threat wasn't to the police or my husband or my neighbors. I called my managing editor, the woman who had given me the job. She was fierce and ambitious, a woman who had worked her way from a trailer park to an executive office. She had a Southern lilt to her voice, and whenever I saw her, some part of me screened that moment in *Gone With the Wind* when Scarlett holds on to that radish and swears that she will never be hungry again. Now I was scared and I wanted contact with someone who would buck me up. If anyone threatening came to Mindi's door, she'd beat the tar out of them and then kick them down the front stoop with her designer heels.

I mention her because whenever I hear a young woman say that she's not a feminist — especially a young college-educated woman with a career — I want to ask her how the hell she thinks she got her education, her job, and her right to vote. It wasn't because of women who shrank from the word "feminist" or disdained it. Many of my mentors were men, but for the most part, women were the ones who gave me the push or the job or the advice I needed. I'm not laboring under some illusion that all women are sisters. They're not. But I was lucky to come of age in a time when many of us thought we were pulling for some collective greater good, for the women who would come after us.

For a time, my newspaper was ruled by an executive editor who had come up the hard way through newsrooms, as a woman in the 1950s and '60s. She was legendary in our state for her foul mouth, her drive, and her news acumen. Deborah Howell was a widow when I first knew her. I remember a story, passed on to me from other reporters, about a fabled camping trip she had made with her husband in the remote wilderness of northern Minnesota, in the million-acre Boundary Waters Canoe Area. He collapsed in the forest — they would later find out he had leukemia — and she had to get him to a doctor. The version of the story I heard had her gathering tree branches and sticks to construct a stretcher and then pulling him through the woods to get help. It wasn't true — the actual story is more prosaic if no less tragic — but my point here is that we all believed it could be true, that this woman the size of a teacup could drag an injured man through the trees to safety. She was small, but her will was gargantuan.

She would sit in her glass office, her desk facing the newsroom, and look over her reading glasses at her staff. If you were a young female reporter and she judged you to be inappropriately attired, you would be summoned for a chat. She had worked too hard to get other women a place in the newsroom for any one female to muck it up by looking less than serious. A friend of mine was pulled into the office once because her earrings were "too dangly." Behind her back, we rolled our eyes, but she had a point. This was in a day when the production guys amused themselves with a motorized toy car with a mirror on it whenever a female editor wearing a dress was on the production floor; whoever had the remote control would try to manipulate the vehicle near the editor's shoes so he could look up her skirt with the mirror. A veteran news reporter thought it was funny to leave the rape-detection kit he got from a cop pal on the desk of a young female reporter. It was the real thing, replete with official forms and the cotton swabs for tissue samples.

One summer, I had interned at a small-town daily that

boasted a popular column by a veteran woman reporter, usually her musings about her family and friends. I didn't think I had much to learn from her; I was hoping to do *real* journalism, you see. At the end of the summer, she offered to take me and the other intern — also female — to lunch. During the meal, she started to reminisce about her early days at the paper, back during World War II, when the men were overseas and she was one of the few reporters in the newsroom. Those were the good old days, she said; she had covered courts and cops and city hall, writing fresh copy for the different editions, switching from crime to political campaigns to tax policy. Her eyes got a little dreamy when she talked about her work, but I remember the way she snapped to reality when she told us what had happened after the war was over. The men got their jobs back and she was demoted.

"What did you do?" I asked.

She shrugged. "I bought a fur coat and I covered weddings."

I wonder now if that lunch was purely a social gesture. I think she wanted us not to take anything for granted. I'm guilty of that sometimes — thinking that my own talent is all I need to get somewhere, which is really just as ridiculous as a twenty-three-year-old law student crinkling her nose and saying she's not a feminist.

Bullshit. I'm here by the power of women who hung on in newsrooms even when they were demoted or laughed at or threatened. When I was a girl, the stories about suffragettes always left me slightly embarrassed and uncomfortable.

Yeah, what they did was great, but did they have to be so weird? And wear bloomers too? Now I marvel at their courage.

Last Christmas Eve, I was escorting my parents out of church after candlelight services when my eyes fell on a pretty blond woman in the back row: Kathy Anderson. We both gave little gasps and burst into tears. She leaned over the pew to hug me and we stood there in wonderment, weeping and shaking our heads. I was still clutching my little snuffed-out candle on its white wooden cross. We walked out of the sanctuary and then stood in a corner, comparing notes. She had been divorced twice and married three times. Her youngest daughter was a junior in college and she had five grandchildren. After many years in Florida, she was back in Moline. I was divorced and had no children and was living in New York and writing a book.

"Do you remember that day we played Barbies for the last time?" I asked her.

"Oh, yes," she said knowingly. "We didn't want anyone to see us."

I felt some relief that she remembered that afternoon as fervently as I did. I think of it now, the pulled shades, the secrecy, those two girls dressing and undressing the dolls, fumbling as they chose the outfits and came up with story lines, none of it enough to prepare them for what would follow.

Newspaper Days

WHEN I WAS A YOUNG REPORTER, I was sent to cover a small Wisconsin town that had been wiped out by a tornado. Almost every building had been smashed in the path of the storm. We were on deadline and the editors had chartered a plane to take us from St. Paul to Madison, Wisconsin; from there, the photographer and I would drive to the site and then get into another plane — this one much, much smaller — so that we could tour the damage and better render the full scope of the tragedy with aerial photos. I was in my tornado gear — rubber boots, rain slicker, extra notebooks stuck in my pockets — and hunkered down in the back of the tiny plane.

I decided to keep my fear of small aircraft to myself.

The devastation was impressive and heartrending. Houses

looked as if their wooden ribs had splintered, with long pieces of lumber and shingles and bricks splattered on the ground. I was taking notes but I was also trying very hard not to get sick. The pilot kept dipping the plane so the photographer could get the angle he wanted. "That's it, that's it, a little more," the photographer said, and with each swoop, I could feel my doughnut and coffee begin their scalding re-entry into my esophagus.

I began to sweat and tried to think of other things. The plane thrummed and went up and down and up and down and my mouth started to flood with bile and I knew from my long history of vomiting during transport that I had better find a repository fast.

Just then the photographer snapped his head back at me — *Thank God,* I thought, *he realizes I'm sick* — and shouted this request: "Can you hold the window open?" He wanted to get his shots without the intrusion of the glass between his lens and the remnants of that little town.

I leaned over to put my hand on the window. The wind hit my face at the same time that the vomit flew out of my mouth, and the force of the rushing air pushed it back in my direction, pelting sour chunks of breakfast at my face and hair until the globs were running down my slicker.

The photographer was good at his job; a little vomit didn't slow him down. Eventually, I had nothing more to spew and sat back, silently praying that we would soon land and trying to control the sharp dry heaves that were shaking my body. I felt something wet between my thighs and wondered if I had spilled something, only to look down and see that blood was seeping through my khaki pants. My period — never wanting to miss a good time — had arrived early.

I asked the pilot if he had any tissues or paper. It didn't seem a good time to ask if he happened to have any tampons on board.

We landed just on the outskirts of the town. I didn't look behind me to see if I had left bloodstains on the plane's upholstery, because I figured the pilot would be occupied enough with the puke on the window. We made our way to what was left of the community, walking down streets that were no longer lined by houses but by foundations. Here and there, a few walls were still standing, as if someone had decided to rip aside a stage curtain and show you the interiors of people's homes. It was eerie.

The Red Cross had already set up a tent, and I went in to see if I could locate the town officials. A kind man saw me and walked toward me holding out a bottle of water, which I gratefully accepted. He didn't say much, just stood there, ready to help, which is not the reception a reporter always gets, and I was starting to feel lucky when it hit me: I was covered in blood, snot, vomit, and tears. He probably thought I was a tornado victim.

Why did I want to be a newspaper reporter?

For the glamour.

My journalism career began in earnest the day I entered the offices of the *St. Paul Dispatch,* an afternoon newspaper that is now no more. It was 1982 and the newsroom was closer in spirit to *The Front Page* than to *Lou Grant.* The copy-desk was staffed almost exclusively by men, one of whom wore a green eyeshade. Long-distance calls were routed by the women at the old-fashioned switchboard in an adjoining room, and more than once, I would be in the middle of a phone interview when I would hear a metallic click and the line would go dead. The next sound on the line would be one of the operators: "Sorry. I'll reconnect you, honey."

The library was still called a morgue. Reporters had to shuffle through thousands of small envelopes that held scissored newspaper clippings, many of them filed under the eccentric system of a long-dead librarian who had maintained his job security by ensuring that no one else could find anything. An example: staff-written articles on Charles Lindbergh, claimed by Minnesotans as a native son because he grew up in Little Falls, were filed under "W" for "World Traveler."

The days when reporters were hired based on their ability to hold liquor were over, but just barely. If someone had told me he had a bottle of hard stuff in the bottom desk drawer, I would have believed him. Ashtrays were fixtures on desks, and I — who had only recently started smoking at the ripe old age of twenty-two, during a newspaper internship in Detroit — made good use of mine. There is a picture of me from those days, with my tightly permed curly hair, cradling a phone between my shoulder and ear, taking a slug out of a can of diet cola, and holding a burning cigarette. I was probably doing the task of cop checks, calling up local police dispatchers to see if they had anything to report. The caption on that photo might as well be HELLO, SWEETHEART, GET ME REWRITE.

I arrived at the *Dispatch* as a freshly minted graduate student of history at the University of Chicago, with an undergraduate degree in journalism from Northwestern University. Sometime during my first few days I made a joke about the transition from reading Spinoza to covering suburban cops. Actually, the closest I had come to Spinoza was to pick up a book, look inside, and quickly switch majors from intellectual history to American cultural history, but I thought my witticism conveyed the change in atmosphere that I had undertaken.

This was a mistake. For months, the favorite sport of the extolled rewrite man, a stone-faced military veteran whose impassivity hid his intellect, was to sit on a corner of my desk and ask me yet again about "that Spinoza fellow." I deserved it.

Another reporter started on the same day that I did, a dark-haired man from Chicago who had trained at the famous City News Bureau and whose nickname was Buzz. He was only a few years older than I was, and he had sharp appraising eyes, an old-fashioned mustache, and an even more old-fashioned and romanticized vision of our profession than I did. He took an immediate dislike to me that day. I think if I could have read his mind, I might have found the phrase "candy-assed, overeducated daughter of privilege."

At the very least, I was far too green a reporter for his taste, and he didn't want to be associated with me. When a city editor gave us a tour of the newsroom, Buzz took pains to walk three steps ahead of me so that I was practically skipping like a schoolchild to keep up. I can only imagine his chagrin when we became deskmates. I sat directly across from him for months, and he eventually treated me as he would a pesky little sister, with a mixture of open contempt and suppressed affection. In the mornings, between our deadlines, we would play hangman, one eye on the clock and with an ear to any editor who might yell out a question or ask what the hell we were doing with all that copy paper.

I learned a lot, not all of it about journalism. There was a newsroom Lothario, of course, who had a silky, reptilian charm, along with a troubled marriage, and I was briefly one of his victims. My just punishment was to sit and watch him on the phone as he wooed his next victim, a reporter who sat one desk away from me. They would talk on the phone in the newsroom, their eyes darting around the bustling office, only occasionally meeting. Finally, fed up, I called his extension one day and asked if he could please have the decency to do his courting somewhere else. He hung up.

I learned to stand up for myself, to take the chaff and ribbing that come with any fraternal occupation. We had a resident dandy who wore three-piece suits and silk handkerchiefs in his breast pockets, with slicked-back curly brown hair and a beau geste profile. One day he stood behind Buzz, rooted around in his trouser pockets, and then withdrew a penny, which he tossed onto my desk.

"Here," he said, "that was for last night."

I looked at him and drew in my breath. "Thanks," I said. "I'm surprised you can find anything when you put your hands in your pockets."

His face reddened and he stalked away. I looked for confirmation at Dewey, one of the quieter editors who sat near me and who had been kind. He was smiling. I was OK.

We were an afternoon newspaper, with editions thumping on people's front porches about the time they were getting home from their day shifts at the breweries and mills and appliance factories. One of my first assignments was to do cop checks from home, meaning I needed to get up before five a.m. to call the various dispatchers at the county sheriffs' offices in the region, trolling for any newsworthy incidents that might have happened overnight. I woke up each morning to a phone call from Irv, a city editor who was steadfast in his habits, wearing the same worn cardigan every day at his desk. He elongated or changed every reporter's name so that his cry on deadline was so distinctive it could not be ignored, sort of the way hunters use different calls for ducks and pheasants and geese. He christened me "Katey," for instance, and I was summoned with "Kaaaaaaaaaaydeeeeeeeeee!"

He used a different tack for his wake-up calls, crooning, "Good morning, beautiful," in his distinctive baritone. I appreciated the gesture, since, by rights, he didn't have to call me and had obviously taken pity on the fact that I had never been a morning person. When he retired a decade later, I brought him a bouquet of red roses and told him that he had been the only man ever to call me beautiful in the morning.

He looked at the flowers, looked at me, and said, "I lied."

I learned to swear like a sailor. Actually, more like a Vietnam-era Marine, since I was lucky enough to fall in with a group of editors and staffers who had done time in 'Nam, as I learned to call it. They taught me how to insert a particularly Teutonic verb into any conversational phrase, e.g., "Ab-so-****-ing-lute-ly your ****ing piece is due for the ****ing peach edition," which for newspaper civilians translates to "Give the finished story to me NOW. It's running in the early edition."

At one point, I proved to be too apt a pupil and was swaggering my way through a homicide office at police headquarters, asking questions about a case, when a savvy detective, a man I admired, said gently, "I wish you would watch your language. We don't talk like that."

He was right, and, abashed, I did as he asked.

I was surrounded by characters who would be edited out of any work of fiction, redlined as unbelievable or clichéd. But we really did have a writer of Irish heritage in the newsroom who made regular visits to a Celtic watering hole rumored to have links to the Irish Republican Army. There really was a monster-motorcycle-ridin', tattooed giant of a photographer who once crossed his mighty biceps and boomed out a warning to a group of angry farmers in overalls who had me backed against a wall at a Farm Aid concert. There really was a graphic artist who paraded around in a leather jerkin and tights, and who carried his violin to the roof and played to the stars during the night shift.

That the place was populated with characters was a given. There was a self-conscious effort in those days to keep alive the spirit of rabble-rousing and individualism that had drawn many of us to journalism in the first place. When I was an intern in Detroit, the self-proclaimed bad seeds among the reporters took over the back third of the newsroom and hung from the ceiling a rubber chicken and a banner that said, ABANDON HOPE, ALL YE WHO ENTER HERE. Who wouldn't want to work with these people?

Newsrooms had generational fault lines, and you could easily distinguish among those who had ended up at the paper before the days of fancy journalism degrees and internships, those who had heeded the calls of the counterculture and New Journalism, and those who had felt the call in the wake of Watergate and the Pentagon Papers. I knew a guy who had gone into reporting after getting his law degree from a prestigious school. His mother traced his decision to the depictions of Carl Bernstein and Bob Woodward by Dustin Hoffman and Robert Redford respectively in *All the President's Men*. He did a terrific imitation of how she would shrug and say to anyone who would question why he had taken such a low-paying career turn, "What can I say? He saw the movie."

That I ended up in the news business is the result of having grown up in unusual circumstances, in a three-newspaper town, so that one paper arrived on our doorstep in the morning and two in the afternoon, newspapers with lovely old-fashioned names such as *The Times Democrat* and *The Daily*

Dispatch. I already had a fondness for the printed word, so I would study the comics pages and the advice columns as well as scrutinize the photos on the engagements and wedding pages. I was a little girl when Robert Kennedy was assassinated, but I can recall very clearly the front-page photo of his corpse on the floor, his eyes seeming to stare right into mine from the paper.

Newspapers taught me about the outside world, and then, when I became a reporter, they thrust me into the outside world. I spent several years covering the crime beat, an education I wouldn't trade for anything now, although it had its moments of tedium.

One of my predecessors at the paper had been a storied legman named Nate Birnbaum, who worked out of his office at the cop shop. What that means is that he called in his notes from his desk at the main police station and someone else wrote the stories. Nate hadn't been gone too long from this world when I took over. A ruler remained in the desk with his name scratched in the wood. Nate had worked at that desk for so long he had practically been a cop himself, and a conversation with him was considered an unofficial part of any training for new officers.

Because I was young and untested and female, I was seen as a bother. Many police officers just looked at me and sighed. Nate's office was directly across the hall from the holding tank for the newly arrested. One of the more constant customers was a recalcitrant street person whose favorite habit was to howl like a wolf until he was released. I would sit at my desk and try to write and make phone calls, staring at Nate's old ruler, listening to the lupine song of the recently incarcerated.

There were just as many characters in the police department as there were in the newsroom. My favorite watch commander read thick tomes of philosophy between emergencies and liked to update me on his renovation of his grandparents' Victorian three-story on the East Side, a storied part of St. Paul. The most voluble of the detectives was a man given to wearing plaid Sansabelt slacks and who kept a glass jar of cigars on his desk.

"Lanpher," he asked me once during an interview about a homicide, "why are martinis like a woman's breasts?"

I don't know.

"Because one's not enough." Here he paused and worked the stogie in his mouth. "And three are too many!"

A suburban chief detective took pity on me and explained the hierarchy of his department and fed me news tips. When I discovered he had multiple sclerosis, I was unabashedly concerned, and his brow furrowed as he ordered me not to make a big deal out of it. One night, he called me with breaking news: a man had holed himself up in his ranch house with a gun, threatening to shoot anyone who came near.

I drove out in the night to the cul-de-sac in question, easy to find with all the squad cars pulled in a semicircle like covered wagons. I parked and went looking for the detective, and when I spotted him, I waved and ran to meet him. He half-tackled me, sending me to the ground. "You idiot," he hissed. "You just ran across the line of fire."

I learned about the use of language by reading police reports of crimes great and small. Sometimes the sparse text of a police report could be as revealing as Chekhov, as mournful as Chandler. The author of a report on a murder-suicide in a suburb called Roseville noted that the husband had killed the wife and then himself in the family room, with his-and-her easy chairs pulled to the fire, her book and his folded newspaper alongside their respective chairs. The neatness of the scene made me wonder what had happened in those moments just before he put down his paper and grabbed the rifle. I carried the picture evoked by that police report around with me for years.

As a journalism student, I found that the moments I struggled most, the moments when my hands froze over the typewriter keys, were those when I had to assemble a disparate array of facts in order of priority. At first, all the details of a shooting or a train wreck or a city-council meeting looked important to me. Who was I to judge? Gradually, through the years, kind editors and impatient ones, born teachers and irascible tyrants, taught me how to string a story together.

I was not a natural journalist. It didn't come easy to me, and a few editors sat me down and urged me to think hard, really hard, about whether this was what I wanted to do. I didn't leave the profession, in part because I was stubborn and didn't want to be seen as a failure. But also in part because to leave would be akin to closing up an adventure tale without finding out what happened next. And, always in my life, I have wanted to find out what happened next.

The first story I wrote that was deemed a success — even the grouchiest of copyeditors liked it — was a profile of the blind owner of a downtown bar that was going to be forced to relocate because the city needed the land to build a new trade center. The bar had once been a house of burlesque, and the owner was a former pro football player who, it was rumored, had been blinded in a shoot-out with a pimp. He had little comment on that but wanted me to know he had been there so long he could still fix the plumbing, just by feel. He knew the pipes. Moving the building would blind him in a way that the gunshots never had.

He was called Al, and he could lovingly recall the acts he used to book into the place: the woman who performed with snakes, the woman who stripped underwater, the woman who walked out onstage as a bum and then revealed herself to be a gorgeous blonde. They were "beautiful girls, beautiful girls," he said. While I talked to him, a bored skinny girl in a string bikini stood atop the wooden bar and listlessly gyrated to music. The regulars, most of them denizens of the senior-citizen high-rise down the street, ignored the dancer, paying closer attention instead to their cups of coffee and the pictures they traded of their grandchildren.

I wondered if Al thought he was still running a fine house of burlesque. He invited me back to watch some old home movies he had taken of the place when he booked rock-and-roll acts, including a local sensation who had opened for Elvis. I watched him thread the film in the projector and nod in time with the tick-ticking sound the spinning wheels made as the film spooled through, black-and-white images moving in a herky-jerky fashion he couldn't see.

When I was a kid, we had this antique contraption at our house called a stereoscope. It was an optical instrument with a long wooden handle, at the end of which you displayed two pictures of the same scene taken from slightly different angles. You viewed them from two lenses, and the effect was that a flat picture was given the illusion of three dimensions.

I stayed in the newspaper game for twenty years because the people there taught me to notice the details in life, the telling details that unfold a story. An eighty-nine-year-old woman tells you about her father's sugar-beet farm, how she learned to knock the beets together to get the dirt off after she pulled them from the ground. A young mother in shock tells you how a tornado blew the bolts out of a door and into her son's forehead, killing him but leaving the door intact and standing in its frame. A blind man looks at an old movie and narrates the action, down to the way someone on-screen does the twist. You become a stereoscope, and all of it, the horrific and the human, is there to be seen.

On Reading

THERE IS A PICTURE OF ME when I was twenty-four, taken
at a party. The last time I saw it was when I threw it, in its
plastic frame, into the trunk of the car during one of my
moves. I don't know where it is now, probably packed away in
a box in my attic in St. Paul. But I don't need the picture in
front of me to tell you what I looked like then. I remember:

Although the movie *Annie Hall* has been out for years, I
still like to dress that way, and I am wearing khaki pants, a
blue checked Brooks Brothers cotton shirt with a contrasting
white collar, a navy cardigan, and a vintage rep tie that I had
found on one of my foraging trips through the antique stores
of Grand Avenue. My skin is smooth, my cheekbones promi-
nent, and my jawline sharp. My hair is short and is a dark seal-
brown, parted on the side. I have a sad, knowing smile, the

way you are sad when you are in your early twenties and feel a little lost, the smile of a young woman who would sit in the dark and listen to Ella Fitzgerald and sip scotch, ruminating on what she was going to do with her life.

I embroider a bit. But when I recall that smile, that's what I think of, the long nights in the dark, the lonely afternoons that stretched before me on the weekends. I had landed a college degree, a master's degree, and a job — not to mention a pile of debt, but that didn't bother me in those days — and now I didn't know what to do with myself. Before, I had always had some sort of academic achievement to run after — a midterm paper, a final exam, an essay for a school application — that could keep me from pondering what I was going to do with the rest of my life. Now the rest of my life was in front of me, and I wasn't sure what to do. When I talked to my friends from college, most of them were busily progressing ahead with life — moving to big cities or getting married or studying for the bar exam. Me, I was sitting in a small apartment in St. Paul, hoping that my next reporting assignment wouldn't be the exhibition of butter sculptures at the state fair.

I would haunt the used bookstore down the street from me, trolling the shelves for books I had meant to read in college. That's how I introduced myself to Thackeray's *Vanity Fair,* to Hermann Hesse's *Steppenwolf,* to *The Tale of Genji.* My reading was promiscuous. I would roll from John Gardner to Charles Dickens to Colette — whatever happened to be on those shelves of worn paperbacks that rang a far-off bell of recognition, of yet another classic that a well-read woman should know. I read Iris Murdoch's *The Nice and the Good* and fell into her net the way I imagine Alice fell through the rabbit hole, swiftly and without much thought. I loved Murdoch's worlds of complicated people and smart conversations, and, lucky me, she had written so prodigiously that I could gobble up book after book. I absorbed every detail I could, and in my inner life, I began to refer to jumpers and crisps, only to be stricken when I finally traveled to London and discovered they were merely sweaters and potato chips. Describing a romantic entanglement to my best friend from college, I said airily, "It's so Murdochian," and my friend, gifted to this day with a fine sense of comic timing, paused a beat and replied, "No, it's more like *Dallas*."

A book gave me someone to come home to. When I think of my twenties and I think of pleasure, what comes readily to mind are those moments when I found a new book or a new author. I was sick with flu one of those winters, floating in and out of a medicated haze, but I had stumbled upon James Crumley and the Vintage paperback of *Dancing Bear*, his homage to Raymond Chandler and Dashiell Hammett set in the Pacific Northwest and centered on a coke-sniffing private detective named Milo. I was in my little apartment on Avon Street in St. Paul, a chopped-up railroad flat.

My bedroom was so small it could fit only a twin bed, so to be properly and luxuriously sick I set myself up in the living room in an old rust-colored velvet recliner handed down from my parents. There I would doze and read, covered to the chin in an afghan knitted by Great-Aunt Kathlene.

I read *Dancing Bear* straight through and later would memorize the first sentence of one of his other novels, *The Last Good Kiss,* a sentence for which I retain my fondness:

> When I finally caught up with Abraham Trahearne, he was drinking beer with an alcoholic bulldog named Fireball Roberts in a ramshackle joint just outside of Sonoma, California, drinking the heart right out of a fine spring afternoon.

I fell in love with James Crumley, with the handsome, craggy face in the author's photo, with a man who could write a sentence like that. I had a crush on him for so long that, years later when he came to St. Paul to do a reading, I drove by the bookstore but couldn't make myself go in. I did it partly out of mercy for me: my crush was so obvious, it might as well have been printed in fourteen-point Helvetica on my face. I also stayed away out of mercy to him: I was fairly certain that no human being could live up to what I had been romanticizing for so long.

During that same bout of flu, I came across a copy of a volume that held all five of Hammett's novels, so while I was sniffling and wheezing and feeling alternately very hot and very cold, I was also awash in the blood of the hard, hard people in *Red Harvest* and immersed in the patter of the speech in *The Thin Man*. When I read the short introductory note by Lillian Hellman, I sighed with jealousy; I read it now and marvel at how completely she had to own him, even in a note long after he was dead. I discovered that Dash Hammett and I had the same birthday, which pleased me immensely. I wanted anything that would grant me closeness to the world of books and authors.

I can tell you exactly when I first voiced that ambition: I had given myself the day to read in bed, reasoning that I would probably never have another chapter in my life with so many empty hours. I imagined myself at some point in the future, a mother teasing and scolding her children, complaining that she never had time to read. "Before you came along," I would tell them, "sometimes I would sit in bed all day and read." It was that afternoon — an overcast day, there was no light cutting through my bedroom window — when I looked up from the wrinkled white sheets and thought, *I want to be a writer.*

On Sundays I would walk to a bookstore and buy a sheaf of reading: the *New York Times,* the *New York Review of Books,* the *Times Literary Supplement* from London. The bookstore was called Odegard's, and when writers came there to read, they would leave their autographs on the walls. I would walk slowly through the store and study the names. Sometimes I would take myself out to brunch at a Filipino restaurant next door where a classical guitarist played. I would listen and eat slowly.

In those days, I read book reviews almost as if they were

guidebooks or maps. I read novels to keep from feeling lonely, to imagine that there were other feet besides mine on the washed wooden floor of my apartment. Sometimes I wondered if it was possible to read too much, if people could use books as a way of evading their day-to-day lives. I read a magazine essay in which the writer posited that she was reading instead of having relationships. I could see the danger of that, wanting to get your workday over with so you could go home to what felt like your real life, the one between the covers of a book. The voices in books filled up my head, competed with one another to narrate the events of the day so that I could turn from a young woman at a dance in Tolstoy's Russia to a man speaking through cigarette smoke in Chandler's Los Angeles to — of course — a woman wearing a jumper and eating crisps in Murdoch's London. I was certain that if I actually opened my mouth, I could parrot any of these people. I kept my mouth shut.

When I was eleven or so, I had hit upon what I thought was a brilliant way to occupy myself during the social calls we would pay to my mother's relatives in the country, throughout which it seemed incumbent upon me to do nothing more than make sure I didn't slide off a slippery sofa or keep to myself the observation that the kitchen sure smelled like cats. I was young and ruthless in my judgments: old people were boring. Their conversations were boring. If I was to be forced along on these social outings, I would do the mature thing and entertain myself. The first time we loaded up the car for one of these family excursions and I lugged a book along, my mother gave me a questioning look. Within our family of four, I was the one who would have been elected Most Likely to Get Carsick While Reading. It was so bad that she always carried a package of Dramamine tablets for me in her purse just in case. But I didn't open the book in the car. I waited until we had established ourselves in the living room of the day's first destination, then flipped open my book and commenced reading, tuning out everything else. This strategy did not go over well. The walk back to the car was accompanied by a scolding. What did I think I was doing? Did I know how rude I was being?

No, I didn't. Up until then, reading had been one of the few pleasures that couldn't be overly indulged, that was never inappropriate, that was often, in fact, rewarded. My mother tells me that one of my favorite toys as a baby was a little cloth book that I would happily hold and chew, gumming the pages. I was already devouring books. When I was in grade school, my name was published in the local newspaper as one of the children who had read the most books that summer during the library's annual reading drive. I ran, screaming with glee, to show the clipping to our next-door neighbors Jonnie and Mickey, who were like an aunt and uncle to me. I made such a commotion that when Jonnie finally came to the door and read the article, she laughed at my excitement over the tiny agate type. I didn't care. I was somebody. I could read.

To say that I loved the children's room of my hometown library would be to understate my true devotion. Erected in

1903, the downtown Moline Public Library was a grand old building with two massive columns on either side of the entrance, one of the hundreds and hundreds of libraries built across the country in the late nineteenth and early twentieth centuries with money from industrialist Andrew Carnegie. The children's room had wooden bookshelves lining the soft butter-colored walls and a cozy-looking brick fireplace. An additional room sat behind the checkout desk; this sanctum was for teachers. I read so much that my favorite librarian let me wander among the stacks back there; I read the teachers' edition of the reading primer for my second-grade class the summer before I started second grade, a liberty that my teacher, Mrs. Gustafson, soon came to rue. I figured this out because of my keen sensitivity to the feelings of others and also because, one day when I was vigorously waving my hands in the air, enthusiastically shouting, "I know the answer! I know the answer! I read the book!" Mrs. Gustafson finally cracked, turned to me, and snapped, "Shut up!"

The name of that favorite librarian is gone from my memory. She looked, to my child's eye, like an illustration, an adult who had stepped out of the pages of *Dick and Jane,* with curled-under brunette bangs and coral lipstick, mock-turtleneck sweaters and wool skirts. She knew a lot about me, like the fact that I loved an old, old book called *Tales of a Chinese Grandmother,* a compendium of fables and fairy tales with a greasy green leather cover. And she knew that I loved Madeleine L'Engle and chocolate, so it wasn't exactly forensic science for her to figure out what happened when a new

L'Engle title — it may have been *A Wind in the Door* — was returned with a smear of chocolate on the frontispiece. She called our house immediately. I pleaded guilty, and oh, it was hard to look her in the eye the next time I saw her. And if you must know, it was a Caravelle bar.

That I would think to combine books and chocolate, well, this one I can put squarely at the feet of my mother. I was five when she took me, with great ceremony, to get my first library card. I checked out five books, one of which was a collection of poems. Then my mother took me to Lagomarcino's, an old family-run confectionery down the street, a place that to this day retains its mahogany booths and Tiffany lamps over each marble tabletop. She ordered my first hot-fudge sundae; the homemade sauce came in a little glass pitcher that you poured over the ice cream scooped into the tulip glass.

Books and hot fudge? The only thing that could be better was what we did next, returning home to take off our street clothes and climb into my parents' bed for a nap together. We kept our slips on, mine out of crinoline and hers out of something silky and smooth. The room was painted a pale green and the beige drapes were pulled to shut out most of the afternoon light. We read and napped until it was time to get ready for supper.

It remains one of the most perfect afternoons I've ever had in my life.

My first year in New York, I found myself reading again with the passion I had had for it in my adolescence and my young adulthood — a passion I thought I had lost. I had hosted a daily public radio show in Minnesota, and while I had got to read more than ever, it was a sort of devil's bargain, and pleasure wasn't in the equation. I hosted two hours of live radio every weekday, with each hour of interviews devoted to a particular topic or book; you had to have some idea of what you were talking about, if only so you could ask sensible questions. I was a fast reader, but even I found it hard to get through the material. Just three days' worth of programming might entail reading an inch-thick stack of articles on agricultural policy; a sociologist's new book on how husbands and wives divide household chores; a sheaf of magazine stories on Warren Beatty's political aspirations; and a new memoir by *Gourmet* editor Ruth Reichl. I couldn't read anymore without wondering which sentence would get to the heart of the subject or narrative, which paragraph I should mark for the author to explicate. Books left my hands ruffled with Post-it notes and weighted with paper clips to demarcate particular pages. I used to joke that my favorite books were by dead authors, since there was no chance I would have to interview them.

There is a bookstore on Bleecker Street in Greenwich Village that is not much bigger than a large closet. It is across the street from a bakery famous for its cupcakes. When I first moved here, I was incredulous that scores of people would line up to pay nearly $2.00 for a cupcake, but the bakery had been featured as a location on *Sex and the City,* and the would-be Carries and Samanthas wait patiently, perhaps pretending that they live in Manhattan. Of course, the New Yorkers I know avoid the place, complaining about the tourists. I watch the cupcake line swell and ebb in size because I am also outside, foraging for books at two outdoor tables covered with remaindered tomes, all judiciously selected. During the winter months, I roll my eyes at people who would stand in line in the cold for a cupcake, but it's quite possible the cupcake people look over at me and wonder why I would stand outside to shop for books.

I do it because I love the serendipity of it, never knowing what I will find among the piles of biographies and translations and memoirs and fiction. I have yet to visit those two tables and not walk away with something I want to buy — the new translation of *Anna Karenina,* the hardcover of last winter's must-have novel, the World War I trilogy by that English author someone told me to read. I was standing at that table not long ago when a young woman's hand reached across mine to pick up a book with Susan Sontag's photograph on the cover.

"Who's that?" I heard a voice say.

"Susan Sontag" was the reply. Then, more diffidently, "She died recently. She was my mother's best friend."

Another time, I was scanning the books outside when an older man in a brimmed hat put a stubby finger on the spine of a book, muttered, "You!" and then stalked on.

I was browsing in that bookstore on a Saturday evening when an acclaimed and pugnacious writer was leaning against the bookshelves in the corner, complaining vocifer-

ously to the clerk about the advance a younger author had received. "Do you know how much money he got? Do you
know how much money he got?" A snort of derision. "Great,
so now he's got the town house in Brooklyn."

During my first summer in New York, I stumbled upon a
paperback collection of the three memoirs of Mary Cantwell, combined under the title *Manhattan Memoir*. She was a
member of the *New York Times* editorial board who had
served a long apprenticeship in the world of women's magazines in the 1950s and '60s. I flipped to the first page of her
second memoir, *Manhattan, When I Was Young*, and was
drawn to her description of the houses in Greenwich Village,
where she had lived and raised her two daughters. She writes
of a house on West 11th Street, and as I first scanned those
words, I was standing on West 11th Street. There is a curious
thrill when an author names a locale or an avenue you know,
as if the landmarks we pass by every day need some sort of
validation in print.

Then I read these lines, in which she recalls yet another
apartment building:

> I turn my head whenever I pass that one, because I
> remember the girl who lived there and she is painful
> to contemplate. One Saturday, shopping at a shabby
> Twenty-third Street A&P, she stuck her hand in the
> meat bin and, awakened suddenly by the sight of her
> long thin fingers poised over a rolled roast, said,
> "How did I get here?" I'm afraid that if I look at that

apartment building I'll reenter it, put her on again, and go back to sleep.

Reading that, I felt a different sensation, something akin to the deliciousness of seeing an address you know in a book, but more piercing. She had listed an emotional address that I knew all too well, the questing plaint of "How did I get here?" I was asking myself that question almost every day that summer, in ways both cosmic and small.

I bought the book and hurried home. I read it as if it were a thriller, I read it the way a child reads a book past her bedtime, the way a subway commuter is locked into a page-turner and misses his stop — with riveted attention and a constant desire to see what happened next. Here she was in her first apartment with her roommate. Here she was in her first job. Here she was getting married. I read greedily, sopping up details such as her lunches at Henry Halper's Drugstore; the brown, black, and white curtains she made for her first apartment as a married woman; the time she lifted Alice B. Toklas out of a gutter during a visit to Paris. Here, I thought, was a life that sounded familiar, a life of ordinary days studded with extraordinary moments, of someone struggling to be and witnessing her own struggle along the way. Her candor about her fears, her depression, her sexual frigidity, made me think she must have been brave. Sometimes I had to put the book down; the story on the pages felt a little too raw. But I always picked it back up. I was reading for pleasure again — and for the company.

I approached the end of the book with some dread — I didn't want to let her go — but it turned out to contain a sentence I would ruminate about for days. In the final pages of her last memoir, Cantwell is in the hospital with an illness she declines to identify. Drowsy with morphine, she thinks back to her arrival in Manhattan not long after she graduated from college:

> . . . when I emerged from a train into Grand Central Terminal, a leather-cased Smith Corona portable in one hand and a suitcaseful of unsuitable — old Bermuda shorts, Brooks Brothers shirts, a gingham skirt, and a dress for after football cocktail parties — clothes in the other. That was the day, I realized on the instant, that I embraced my true bridegroom. That was the day I married New York.

Cantwell died two years after that memoir was published. She was sixty-nine. I read that final passage to a friend once, blinking back tears. "She must have known she was dying," I said. My friend was not as moved as I was, but she was kinder than some of the critics, one of whom had written, "Cantwell proclaims unconvincingly that her real love is the New York she left her Rhode Island family for right after college. . . . It is Cantwell's inability to learn from her past that makes this memoir disappointing."

I wasn't disappointed. I was convinced. For me, it was enough for Cantwell to say that she had made her way through the grids of streets and plats of buildings, only to look back and realize that her one faithful partner in this endeavor was the city itself, in its multitudes and in its isolations.

And I thought of her when I began this endeavor, the writing of these pages. I remember emerging from a publisher's office on Sixth Avenue into a bright sun, my eyes blinking at the sudden light and at the thought that I might write a book. I felt like a bride.

Housebound

I HAD A HOUSE ONCE. I love it still, but I'll probably never live there again. It sits on a little hill on a block of other fine houses in St. Paul, just a street away from Summit Avenue, a long boulevard of grand old mansions and homes. My house, built in 1914, isn't a showcase, but the dining room has a built-in buffet with leaded windows, and the long living room is anchored by a brick fireplace and stained glass windows featuring bright yellow tulips. The heart of the house is the front porch, a long, wide room with mullioned windows that open up to screens on three sides. I had a small wicker dining set out there and a wicker chair and love seat that grew shabbier with use each year. I tracked the porch seasons by what I put in a tall vase by the door, roses and lilacs in the spring, tall gladiolas in the summer, and chrysanthemums in the fall.

Four bedrooms and a sunporch make up the second floor. I turned the sunporch into my office, with two walls of windows overlooking my garden. In the winter, I could watch the cardinals, scarlet against the snow and bare branches. The garage is a small jewel, with fine woodwork on the inside and cream-colored stucco walls on the outside. It looks like a small cottage, with roses and clematis trained on a trellis. When V and I bought the house, the third floor was ripe for renovation, and we found out later from a neighborhood informant that our home had been used once as a boardinghouse, probably back in the 1940s. You can see the vestiges of those days on the third floor, the tattered brown-and-yellow wallpaper, the silent, nonworking radiators still stationed at their posts. There are four rooms on that floor, including a cedar closet. A window in the tiny room at the front holds the best view in the house, a bird's-eye sweep of the surrounding blocks, roof after roof unfolding in front of you, russet-colored tiles, gray-and-brown shingles, the points and corners of gables and eaves, all capping houses like ours, houses that either sheltered children or were meant to have children in them soon.

Oh, yes, the children. We bought the house for the children. I liked the basement, because it had a cement floor painted red, and I could envision my children riding their tricycles down there in the winter, just as I did when I was a kid, stir-crazy in January. I was divided about which room would be best for the first child. Maybe the smallest bedroom, and then when she — the first was always a she, I don't know why — grew older, I would give up my office and let her use it as a playroom, and make the adjoining room her bedroom. Once she grew out of her crib, she could have the antique twin bed that I had bought from one of my parents' neighbors for my first apartment; even then, we all agreed it would make a fine bed for a little girl someday.

See, I was trying to look ahead.

The house was a little bit more than we could afford, but I thought we would grow into it, both financially and physically. Eventually, of course, we would have to put carpet on the wood stairs, the better to cushion the falls of the toddlers. Maybe we would put back the doorway that had been walled over between the kitchen and the stairs, so it would be easier to yell up to sleepy kids in the morning that they had better come downstairs right now, do you hear me? Once we scraped together the money, we could restore the third floor to make a guest suite for my parents, with a private bathroom for when they came to visit their grandchildren.

I had it all planned out.

There is the guilt, for one thing, when you arrive at midlife without a child. Because, honey, if you say you want a child in this day and age, you can have one. If you are a woman of a certain income and education level, there is virtually nothing to stand in your way. You can find a partner who wants to donate his sperm, you can be artificially inseminated, you can get donor eggs, you can adopt domestically, you can adopt internationally, you can adopt a child with special needs, you can marry a man with children and become a stepmother.

In fact, even if you're not a woman, there is nothing to stand in your way. A good friend of mine from college who lives in Hell's Kitchen had been saving his money and planning for his fatherhood for years. When the right man didn't come along in his life, he decided to become a parent on his own. He did the research, found the right clinic, picked donor eggs from a catalog, hired a surrogate mother to carry the fetuses to term, and now is the biological and custodial father of a two-year-old daughter and a newborn son. I have watched him in action with his children, burping his son after a meal, coaxing his daughter to bedtime. I've seen him do the single-parent dance, when both kids want attention and he has one slung over his shoulder and another attached to his hip.

We used to joke back when we were in college that if we were both single when we hit forty — we thought that was old — we would get married and live in a penthouse in Manhattan. Well, we're both past forty now and single. I'm living in two rooms in the Village and he's living in a duplex apartment with a crib and a bassinet, and two roommates under the age of three named Julia and Jackson.

I admire him. I'm just not sure I can emulate him.

When the doctor told me that V and I were infertile as a couple, she was so cheery and upbeat about the available treatments that what she said didn't hit me until I left the clinic: we couldn't get pregnant on our own. I suspect her upbeat presentation was on purpose. She surely didn't relish the duty of telling another woman that she couldn't conceive. I cursed the year and a half I had spent monitoring my cycle, taking my temperature each morning, and charting it in pencil on a graph next to our bed. It had been a waste of time.

Mostly, I was angry that we had lost time and that I had felt so hopeful. Whenever I had noticed an uptick in my temperature, whenever I had looked at the written record, I had thought that somehow I was becoming more intimate with my body's own tidal pulls and waves. It was like finding out you had believed a liar.

When I got home that day, I went straight to the kitchen table, put down my head, and sobbed. The table was from my childhood. My parents had found it in one of their first apartments, left behind by the previous tenants. My mother refinished it, stripping the paint and sanding it, giving it a new coat of varnish. It's pine, stained a light brown and stippled with the whorls and lines of the wood's grain. My parents gave it to me when I set up my first apartment; I had liked the idea of raising my own children around this table.

V came home for an hour's dinner break and I told him the news. I found myself aping the doctor's rah-rah spirit: We're infertile, honey! But it's OK! Science has a cure!

I wonder if V feels now that he had believed a liar.

*   *   *

The Year of Living with Infertility was actually longer than a year, but that's how I think of it, our own version of *The Year of Living Dangerously*. I snapped at people. I burst into tears at every TV commercial with a baby. There were a lot of them. Magazine ads with babies were everywhere. Whenever I went to the doctor's office, there were back issues of *Parent* magazine, and I would pick them up, just so, you know, I would be ready. I read about colic and teething and constipation. I wondered what it would be like to use those tiny scissors to clip those first fingernails and toenails. I read about stretch marks and episiotomies and epidurals. I knew I would breast-feed and was grateful that I could work at home most of the time so that I wouldn't have to use the breast pump in a bathroom stall at the office. I worried that I might not be able to breast-feed. I worried about how I was going to lose all that pregnancy weight.

I thought about all those years in my twenties when I would pray after sex that I wouldn't get pregnant. I thought about all the times in the first few years of our marriage when V and I had made love and I would stay up long after he went to sleep, worried that I would become pregnant and how it would affect my career. Was it time? "It's never the right time," my female colleagues with children said. "Just do it."

Well, it turns out it isn't that easy. To just do it.

I began to notice how many newspaper stories there were on teenage moms, drug-addicted moms, abusive moms, crazy moms. And this is what I wanted to know: if a fifteen-year-old crack-addicted, abused prostitute could get pregnant, why couldn't I?

You realize that you are jealous of fifteen-year-old crack-addicted, abused prostitutes; you realize *Yes, I am living dangerously.*

You realize People Say the Darnedest Things.

In the year after my brother died, I had only one dream in which he appeared to me. This troubled me. Why wasn't I seeing him more? Every now and then, during my waking hours, I would think I spied him in a crowd or walking toward me on the street. But those illusions never lasted long. The only time he appeared in my dream, he was a young boy, skinny, standing in front of the open refrigerator door. It was night and the refrigerator light illuminated his body. I watched him as he looked over the inventory of my refrigerator shelves the way young teens graze with their eyes. He was hungry and I wanted to feed him.

Maybe that is how I gained more than twenty pounds in the year after he died. I look back and realize that the dream was no mystery. I was the one standing there in front of the fridge. I ate without thinking, I ate mechanically, I ate and ate and ate. That dream might have been John's way of saying, "Hey, Sis, step away from the food."

St. Paul has a complicated series of skyways that connect buildings downtown so you don't have to go outside in the often-subzero cold. I was walking down one of those sky-ways that year when I ran into an editor who had first hired me at the newspaper. He had since retired. He saw me ap-proaching him, and as I grew closer, his face took on a warm and paternal smile.

He looked at my thickened middle, lifted his eyebrows, and leaned in to ask, "Are you expecting?"

"No," I said matter-of-factly, "just fat."

His face fell. I walked on.

He was a kind man and I know he didn't mean me harm. Years after that encounter, I found myself made uncomfort-able by the related question "Do you have children?" It came up at dinner parties and other social gatherings, whenever I met new people. I began to hate new people. I was of child-bearing age, I told myself, and I was married, so it was nor-mal for people to ask if I had procreated. But I resented it, I resented the hell out of it.

I practiced different answers. I worked to keep my voice level and unaffected, to respond with a simple and gracious "No." I came up with a cheery, attagirl answer: "Not yet!" I hoped it implied a lot of spunk and longing: *You'll root for me, won't you?* I tried for a modest and mournful sound, some-thing that hinted you shouldn't ask any more questions: "No, sadly, no."

Finally, I realized that the best way to deflect any uncom-fortable conversation was simply to turn the question around: "I bet you're a parent!" Even so, there were people who wanted to know more: Was I trying? Was I infertile? What seemed to be the problem? Was it me? Was it my husband? Which doctor were we seeing? Had we thought about adoption? Did I know that their neighbor's cousin's dentist had a sister who couldn't conceive, and then the same day she and her husband went to pick up their baby from Guatemala, she found out she was pregnant?

Eventually, I came up with the perfect answer that stopped people cold and changed the subject fast. I was at a dinner party when I tried it out for the first time. "Do you have children?" someone asked me.

"No," I said, and smiled. "I'm barren."

Sometime in the midnineties, I am having dinner with two friends from college and we are talking about our lives, what we hope to do in the future.

"What about you?" asks Carolyn, who has a son and three daughters.

Elaine, who has two sons, looks at me, waiting for my answer.

"Oh, there's a lot I want to do — I want to write books, I want to have children," I say.

There is the slightest of pauses.

"Did you notice," says Carolyn carefully, "that you said you wanted to write books before you said you wanted children?"

It's true. I waited to have children. I waited too long. I still believe that I would have been a terrible mother in my twenties. For one thing, I was single, and even if you were a movie star, it was hard two decades ago to have a child out of wedlock and be socially acceptable. If I had become pregnant in my early to midtwenties, I am pretty sure I would have had an abortion. I would have been too afraid of the judgment that would have come crashing down on me.

A few years ago, my parents and I were discussing the plight of a family we knew who had what used to be called an "illegitimate child." My father turned to me and said that he was grateful I had been such a responsible young person. "I'm just glad that you didn't bring shame on the family," he said.

I was shocked. What I wanted to say — but didn't — is that it would have been worth it so that I could have been a mother. And what I wanted to say — but didn't — is that he would have loved that child no matter how she came into the world.

I'm sure of it.

V and I found a fertility doctor who spoke French. To be precise, I found a fertility specialist who spoke French. I thought it would help V feel as if he were part of the process. We scheduled appointments so he wouldn't miss any rehearsals or shows or hours in the shop building sets. By this point, I was so used to his schedule — and to our unspoken agreement that he was making Art, and Art was the priority — that I acquiesced with little argument.

We borrowed money from his mother and from my parents. We set up a payment schedule with the clinic. We went in for the formal interview, where they determine if your relationship is strong enough to go through the rigors of infertility therapy. Sitting through that interview reminded me of the session we had with an immigration official after we got married. We had a funny bureaucrat whose face pulled into a smile when we walked into his office. We sat down and he looked through our papers.

"So," he said, pointing first to me and then to V, "you're a newspaper reporter, you're thirteen years younger, he's a French artist. What do you guys have in common?"

I gave him my answer without even thinking.

"We argue a lot."

I think that convinced him we weren't a sham marriage.

During the infertility interview, we hold hands. We talk about our shared goals. We talk about the stress of infertility. We talk about how this process is testing our relationship. We talk about how we are talking more.

What we don't tell the woman who is interviewing us, the woman with the clipboard, is how for most of our marriage he is home only one night a week, and that, sadly, is the same night as *Monday Night Football*. We don't say how, even now, he works close to eighty hours a week; how afraid I am that I am the third priority in his life, after the theater and his elderly mother. I don't blurt out how I wake up sometimes in a cold sweat, convinced that if we have a child I will slip down to fourth place, that I will be erased, that I will end up a single parent within a marriage, that I will be alone. I keep to myself that I imagine our marriage as a house with fissures in the foundation, cracks that our infertility is slowly making wider and wider.

We pass the infertility interview.

One of the nicest compliments I ever received during my newspaper career was when a colleague, a mother of two, stopped me in the hallway and told me that she liked my column so much she hoped I would become a mother myself someday. I looked at her inquisitively. "I just want to see what you would write about it," she said. "I think it would be really interesting."

I probably would have written something about the anger I saw in so many of the new mothers in my life. It scared me. Some of my friends seethed at the inequity of the work distribution at home, how even the "good dads" just didn't get it. They were angry about the expectations that hemmed them in with so little assistance. We were the generation of American women learning that you couldn't have it all and that many of us couldn't even have most of it.

I was afraid to be that angry. As it was, I was pretty pissed off.

We schedule the first in vitro treatment for a week in June. As it turns out, that is also when V is planning to leave for France to visit his mother, as he does each summer. We sit in the office of a clinic administrator, we leaf through the calendar together, we pick the dates.

When V and I get home, I sober up. I sit him down and explain that if the treatment takes and I become pregnant and he isn't there, I will be angry. And if the treatment doesn't take and I'm not pregnant and he isn't there, I will be angry.

I don't want to be alone.

He says he understands. He says we should reschedule. He says we should wait until fall.

I nod, but I don't really see him because I am beginning to float. I am having an out-of-body experience. I can look down and see the two of us in our living room, I can see him in the chair by the fireplace. I am like an untethered balloon, floating away from this marriage, floating now over the neighborhood rooftops. Soon V will lose sight of me completely as I drift far away above all these houses that were meant to hold children.

In less than a year, he moved out of the house. *Let's be practical,* I said, *I can more easily afford the mortgage on my own.* But my desire to stay in the house wasn't driven by pragmatism, it was emotional. As long as I was in the house, the dream stayed alive: I might raise children there. The house, I argued to myself, had been more constant than he had. Never mind that, at the end of the marriage, I was the one who had sought comfort with someone else. When it was suggested during the course of our divorce counseling that we sell the house, I became so distraught that I found myself one night moving from room to room, weeping, stroking the wallpaper, running my hands over the woodwork.

V was generous. We came up with a solution that allowed me to stay. The relief I felt was palpable.

When I was deciding whether to get a divorce, a friend told me I should just go ahead and have a baby. I was shocked. Wouldn't it be wrong to go ahead and have a child with a man you knew you weren't going to stay with? My friend just shrugged. After all, I said I wanted a child.

After the divorce, I thought about adoption. I went to a financial consultant, a warm and generous woman I just adored. We went over my financial situation, prepared a range of budgets, studied the programs I had researched.

"Let's look at all the options," she said sprightly. "Is there a man in your life who could get you pregnant?"

I sputtered a reply. Sure, but —

"I said we would look at all the options," she said calmly, and then gestured at the papers on her desk. "And it would be a lot cheaper."

In the end, I wasn't sure I was cut out to be a single mother. I had always envisioned that I would raise a child with a partner, and while I had a strong circle of good friends, I didn't look around me and see the extended family I thought I would need to raise a child by myself.

And, yes, as the years go by, sometimes I think my friend was right. I should have gone ahead with the infertility treatment, just had the baby when I was married, even knowing that I was going to divorce the father.

When I think about motherhood these days, the picture that always springs into my mind is that of a window. When I was younger, that window of opportunity was wide open, the breeze flowing through it. These days, the window is almost touching the sill, and it appears to be closed. But look — if you put your hand up to it, you can still feel a little trickle of air.

I haven't given up the dream yet, not completely. There are days when my body literally aches for a child. I can feel the longing in my arms, and sometimes I swear I can feel the same intimacy with my body that I knew when I was tracking my cycle, that knowledge of my own physical self and its calendar.

That meeting with my doctor, the first time we heard that we were infertile, took place in the fall. A few weeks later, I was home carving pumpkins into jack-o'-lanterns for Halloween, my hands orange and slick with the stringy flesh, my fingers scooping out all those seeds, handfuls of seeds. It's a strange custom, when you think about it, to clean out a fruit and then light it, the better to attract children to your door. It was only later that I thought about all those seeds, glistening with life, and how I just threw them away. The waste of it now could strike me down.

I'm in Peru, on a magazine assignment, on a train traveling from the village of Machu Picchu back to the town of Cuzco. The crags of mountains fill up the windows on my left; on my right, I can see long stretches of what looks to be farmland. People are working in the fields, burros standing nearby with packs. When the train runs through villages, you see the backs of houses and makeshift shelters. People turn and wave, faces pop up above windowsills. In a few villages, when the train slows down, packs of children flock to the track and, running alongside the train, hold their arms up to the people in the cars, shouting in English, "Money! Money! Money!" Their smiles are so endearing and they are laughing while they beg, but I find I am angry at the people who throw them coins, angry that this is how these children are learning English, needing only three phrases and two strong legs to complete their transaction: Money! Thank you! Bye-bye!

I know that you don't necessarily have to raise a child to help a child, that maybe some of us are meant to be custodians in the larger sense of the word, the larger sense of the world too. I envision children running alongside that train not to catch coins but because that is what children do, run after things they can't always catch, just to feel their legs pump and their bodies work, just for the joy of it. As I sit in that train, I feel something happening to me, like tectonic plates shifting in my heart. My pocket epiphany from a train ride in Peru is this: You should take the time you have left and mother the world, as much of it as you can. There are so many little arms reaching up to so many trains.

Voice Lessons

WHEN I WAS A LITTLE GIRL, I talked too fast. Way too fast. My brain would rush ahead of my mouth in leaps and bounds, and my tongue would try to keep up, and the next thing you knew I was spouting a dialect that only I could understand, the words all mashed together with no breathing room in between. This rendered communication at home difficult. My parents could have sent me to a speech therapist. Instead, to my everlasting gratitude, they sent me to a former vaudevillian who had set up shop as an elocution teacher across the river in Davenport, Iowa.

Mary Fluhrer Nighswander was a tiny woman with snow-white hair that she wore in a chignon. She kept a picture on her desk of the time she had starred in a production of *Life with Father.* She ran a children's theater as well, and one summer I was cast in a production as a princess; we did boffo box office at several playgrounds. But the picture that remains central in my memory is that of a typical elocution lesson. My mother would drop me off on an early winter's evening in front of the stone steps of the Lend-a-Hand Club, a down-at-the-heels structure near the banks of the Mississippi in downtown Davenport. I would cross the large main floor, darkening with the shadows of dusk, passing the same group of old men dozing in easy chairs next to the unlit fireplace. I never knew if they were lending a hand or receiving one. Mrs. Nighswander's office was on the second floor, and after the grim sitting room below, her brightly lit chamber looked cozy and welcoming. There, I would stand before her and recite some ancient chestnut of verse, such as James Whitcomb Riley's ode to Little Orphan Annie:

> *Little Orphant Annie's come to our house to stay,*
> *An' wash the cups an' saucers up, an' brush the crumbs away,*
> *An' shoo the chickens off the porch, an' dust the hearth an'*
> *sweep,*
> *An' make the fire, an' bake the bread, an' earn her board an'*
> *keep.*

With Mrs. Nighswander in attendance, you learned how to slow down, how to breathe, how actually to speak the poem without falling victim to its singsong rhythm. Chewing gum was forbidden in her office, but there was a gum-ball machine in the lobby of the Lend-a-Hand Club, and most weeks it was just too tempting to see if I could get through the entire poem without her discovering that I had a red gum ball tucked in my cheek. Demosthenes had his pebbles, after all. When people ask me how I ended up in radio, I always think of her, the woman who made sure I had a voice people could understand.

The formal beginning of my radio days was not an auspicious one. I had been a guest on a morning show on KSTP-AM 1500, a 50,000-watt station that broadcast throughout the Twin Cities metropolitan area, and when I walked out of the booth, the station manager asked if I had ever thought about guest-hosting one of their shows. I was a newspaperwoman through and through, and had not once considered a career in broadcasting. But there were enough similarities in radio — after all, it's the words that matter, not how you look — that the prospect sounded inviting. The station arranged for me to guest-host a talk show on the Friday night of Memorial Day weekend, a time slot where I could do the least damage.

The responsibilities of a guest and a host on a talk show are not that dissimilar to the responsibilities of a guest and a host at a dinner party. As a guest, you are expected to show up at a reasonable hour, make conversation, and contribute something to the evening. As a host, you must welcome your guests and make sure that everyone is comfortable, and that no one even suspects that your oven just broke down, the kids threw the hamster in the upstairs toilet, and your husband decided that very evening to start repairing the shingles on the roof.

The home for KSTP-AM in the mid-1990s was a brick Art Deco building from the 1920s lodged out in a field in a St. Paul suburb. It was funny to look at that structure — about the same vintage as the bungalows in my neighborhood, if a little bigger — and think of the disparate voices that would issue forth: Rush Limbaugh, for one, and a host of local voices, including the man for whom I was substituting, a blind and barrel-chested character who called himself The Round Mound of Sound and who played up his handicap, once pitching at a minor-league baseball game.

If you were on the air during the evening shift, the building was pretty much abandoned. It would be you, the producer, and maybe someone from the cleaning crew. There were those of us who preferred it that way. Radio is a personal medium, after all: you're perched on someone's shoulder, talking just to him, sharing stories with only her.

You do have to overcome your awe at the actual technology that carries your voice, however, and that was the problem with my first night on the air as a host. I couldn't get over the fact that if I didn't speak, nothing came over the airwaves. I could say a sentence and hear it through the headphones, and if I didn't say anything else, "dead air" would prevail. Fascinating. I opened my mouth and there was sound. I closed it and there was silence. Not just for me but for anyone tuned in for miles and miles and miles. The implications of this fact made my bowels freeze. Time can slow down on the air, and if you have nothing to say, ten seconds can seem like an eternity. For a while there, I just kept repeating the phone number for listeners to call in, and I would answer the on-air phone lines with fervent prayers that someone else had something to say. This was in the days before the ubiquity of cell phones, so when a friend of mine driving to his cabin took pity on me, he had to pull over to a roadside pay phone. But he called, bless him. At some point, a picture flashed in my mind, a scene from some old World War II movie I had seen, with planes going down in flames and a pilot urgently radioing, "Mayday! Mayday!" I still think of that night and see myself as a burning plane, spiraling nose-down to the ground.

After my stint on the air, I went to a party at a friend's house, relieved that my debut was behind me and comforted by the notion that it couldn't possibly have been as bad as I thought. My hostess opened the door. She winced.

Here is what I love about radio: the velvet intimacy of it, the theater of it, the way you are talking to just one person and to hundreds of thousands of people at the same time. How it is both a performance and the truest thing you'll ever do, because everything is bound up in your voice. No matter how much training you have to iron out your vowels, muffle your accent, starch your consonants, something ineffable and human remains and travels over the air. People love you or hate you based on your voice, and there's not a damn thing you can do about it.

I improved after my first disastrous session on the air and eventually was offered my own call-in show on week-nights. My on-air colleagues included a former Minneapolis city councilwoman who was also the ex-wife of our sitting governor; she liked to tell everyone her pet name for an inti-mate part of his anatomy (if you must know, it was Oscar). Then she would sit back and do a rapid-fire analysis of the lat-est tax bill. Barbara Carlson was the first policy shock jock I had heard, and she would broadcast on Fridays from a hot tub in her backyard. Then there was our morning-drive host, a professional-wrestling star and former mayor of a Min-neapolis suburb. Jesse Ventura and I liked to tease and poke fun at each other; we got along just fine. It was hard to switch gears, however, when he was elected governor in a third-party upset that seemed to delight the nation. By then, I was hosting a sober-minded public radio show. After our first on-air interview, after the cameras and security personnel had left the studio, the vice president for news pulled me aside in the hallway, his mouth turned down.

"Katherine, we call him Governor Ventura. We don't shake our heads and say, 'Jesse, Jesse, Jesse.'"

Oh.

One of the popular weekend shows at KSTP took calls about the great outdoors — a deeply ingrained preoccupation in the Upper Midwest. The two hosts were nicknamed Fish and Bear. Fish looked like the sportsman version of Don Johnson, and Bear looked like a clean-shaven grizzly. They joined me one night for a live broadcast from an ice-fishing shack on an undisclosed lake. As far as I know, it was the first time that someone had been introduced to the sport on-air or, for that matter, had broadcast the sounds of three people fishing on radio. As part of the ice-fishing tutorial, Bear pulled out a small plastic tub of bait.

"Now these are maggies," he told me with a fond, instructional air. "You're gonna have to put them in your mouth to warm them up, because they got frozen."

"You do?"

"Yeah," he said, opening his mouth with a finger. "You put 'em right here, between your lip and your gum."

So I did, prompting an explosion of laughter from both men that probably ruined the eardrums of everyone listening. Maggies, in case you don't know, are maggots. And you don't need to warm them up before they are lowered into the ice-cold water.

I quit my first stint on commercial radio after only sixteen months. I had been doing the show in addition to my thrice-weekly newspaper column, and I felt too tautly stretched. Despite support from management, I didn't fit in at the station. The marketing staff tried their best to promote my talk show, but they needed something: a slogan, a snappy line that would fit on a T-shirt. That was part of the problem: I didn't want to be summarized by anything that would fit on a T-shirt.

Then too I was the lone liberal on a station heavily weighted toward the other end of the political scale. Most people listen to talk radio to have their beliefs confirmed, not challenged. Simply stating that I believed in paying taxes would prompt a flurry of angry callers eager to denounce me as a commie. At first it was amusing. But eventually, when you spend day after day with people so firmly entrenched in their ideology that they will brook no argument or debate, it's not fun, it's just fatiguing.

I call it the Venal Zone, and you can tell you are in it when you hear a certain rasp or sibilance entering into a caller's speech. You start to feel the hate. Also, I was on the air during the ascendancy of Rush Limbaugh, when the word "liberal" was being twisted into an ugly epithet. To be fair, I would like to point out that the Venal Zone is not the exclusive territory of the far right. Years after I left KSTP, I ran into my old boss, the station manager who had first put me on the radio. Now he was running an Air America station and I was traveling cross-country with *The Al Franken Show*. I shook my head in disbelief when I saw him and started to laugh.

"What's it like to go from running a Rush Limbaugh station to running an Air America station?" I asked.

He looked me dead in the eyes. "It's exactly the same," he said. "The people are just at the other end of the political spectrum, that's all."

*   *   *

Little more than a year after I first left commercial radio, I found I missed spinning conversations and taking phone calls. Ask anyone who has been on-air: radio is an addictive medium. So when I heard that Minnesota Public Radio had hired the guy who had founded National Public Radio's *Talk of the Nation* — my favorite show — to run its news division, I decided to take action. In a five-minute burst of self-esteem, I called his new office and left a voice message informing him that I was a newspaper columnist with radio experience and that he should hire me.

To my utter astonishment, Bill Buzenberg called me back. Six months later, I was the host of the weekday call-in show *Midmorning.*

In the beginning, Bill was the only person in the building who thought I was suitable to host a public radio show. Apparently, between my newspaper columns and my show on KSTP, I had acquired a reputation for brashness. Well, I had learned my way in radio from a gang that included a professional wrestler turned politician, a woman who liked to carry dildos and broadcast from a hot tub, and a man who asked me to put maggots in my mouth. To which my response remains, *What's not to like?*

Improbably or not, the show clicked. The ratings went up. I was given a new round of voice lessons — this time no one asked me to recite James Whitcomb Riley — and I learned to concentrate on what I thought I was best at anyway: asking questions. I didn't have to worry about coming up with a one-liner that defined me and my show. There was no such thing as a *Midmorning* T-shirt.

My favorite shows had writers in the guest chair. One day, Robert Bly came by to talk about a new book. While many people associate his name with the men's movement and his bestseller *Iron John,* he is also widely regarded as a poet and translator. We wandered on to the subject of his late friend and fellow poet James Wright, who had come to stay with Bly and his family during the late 1950s. Wright's popular poem "A Blessing" came out of that stay, and I asked Bly to read it.

Just off the highway to Rochester, Minnesota,
Twilight bounds softly forth on the grass.
And the eyes of those two Indian ponies
Darken with kindness.
They have come gladly out of the willows
To welcome my friend and me.

The "friend" was Robert Bly. As he began to reminisce about the car trip that led to that poem, I was suddenly struck with an ineluctable gratitude. This, I told myself, is like sitting down with a great Shakespearean author recalling the time when old Will saw a rose and was inspired to write a love sonnet. I motioned for Bly to keep reading.

We step over the barbed wire into the pasture
Where they have been grazing all day, alone.
They ripple tensely, they can hardly contain their happiness
That we have come.
They bow shyly as wet swans. They love each other.
There is no loneliness like theirs.
At home once more,
They begin munching the young tufts of spring in the darkness.
I would like to hold the slenderer one in my arms,
For she has walked over to me
And nuzzled my left hand.
She is black and white,
Her mane falls wild on her forehead,
And the light breeze moves me to caress her long ear
That is delicate as the skin over a girl's wrist.
Suddenly I realize
That if I stepped out of my body I would break
Into blossom.

I began to weep, and I pulled back from the microphone because I didn't want anyone to know. Bly smiled and said, "I just want everyone to know that Katherine is crying." Tears were rolling down my face. At that moment, I could hardly contain my happiness.

I ended up at Air America Radio not because of my political beliefs but because of my fondness for Bob and Ray, the classic radio-comedy duo. I was hosting *Midmorning* and compiling research on a guest — his name was Al Franken — when I stumbled on the transcript of a speech Al had given at the National Press Club. The subject was the evils of predatory lending, and he had used an old Bob-and-Ray bit to ensure that people listened.

To this day, that's something I love about Al, that he can make you laugh and think about economic inequity at the same time. During a break in our interview, I told him I had read his speech and admired how he had worked in Bob and Ray. "You're my kind of people," he told me warmly at the end of the show.

I'd like to think he said it because I had done such a good job of researching his background. He'll tell you it's because I laughed so hard at his jokes.

We first started talking about his Air America show more than a year before it launched. I was visiting New York and met him for coffee to try to talk him into taping a pilot for public radio. His response surprised me: he wanted to talk me into joining him to launch a new network. He described the show he wanted to do, the kind of cohost he was looking for, and I laughed.

"What?" I said scornfully. "You want me to be your sweater girl? Like on some 'Morning Zoo' radio show?"

"Well," he said solemnly, "it *is* between you and Carmen Electra." He said he wanted a sidekick like Robin Quivers on *The Howard Stern Show*. "I need someone to keep me honest." My immediate reaction was *no*. Then a friend counseled me to think again: "You don't even listen to that show. How would you know what she does? Robin Quivers is very important to that show."

She also reminded me that I had been casting about for a change. And the more I thought about it, the more interesting the prospect seemed: to launch a new national network that would combine the zip and humor of *The Daily Show* with the social issues and gravitas of public radio, in an effort to bring some philosophical balance to the commercial airwaves. As the months went by, I checked the roster of other Air America hires, which included staffers from CNN, *The Daily Show*, CBS, and public radio. Even employees of Fox were sending in their résumés.

When the job offer came in January 2004, I decided to turn my life upside down. *How bad could it be?* I thought.

It turned out to be more complicated than good or bad.

The early days were hectic. We had only about six weeks to finish hiring the staff, design the format, begin rehearsals, train producers, book guests, set up comedy skits, and make Al a radio star. What bothered me wasn't so much the chaos inside our unit — that was to be expected, we were launching a new show on a new network — but the chaos elsewhere in the organization. Who was the genius who decided to name the network after an infamous CIA operation in Laos? When were we going to get actual offices? Why was it so hard for other shows on the network to find rehearsal spaces? After we got the network off the ground, matters didn't improve. What were these rumors about unpaid bills? About paychecks that bounced? Even Al couldn't get straight answers.

Whenever I turned to other people in the organiza-tion — people who had worked on network or cable TV or commercial radio — they said, "It's a start-up. You're not used to it. This is what life is like when you work at a start-up." Then the financing crashed and the company couldn't make payroll and the news hit the press. I turned to one of the many people who had reassured me that all the mishaps were typical. "Is this normal for a start-up?" I asked. No, it wasn't.

At times during my first year in New York, I felt as if I were living the script of a chick-lit novel, despite the fact that I was fifteen years older than the genre's usual protagonist. The day the financial crisis hit, the book jacket would have read something like this: *Katherine thought she was leaving the Mid-west for a new life in Manhattan, taking on a wacky but beloved boss who wanted not only to save the free world but to put on a ra-dio show too. . . . But what does she do when she discovers that sometimes when you make a bet for a better life . . . you lose?*

Six hours after I discovered I may or may not have a job, a stylist was back-combing my hair and insisting that I try on false eyelashes made of mink. I was going to the season-opening gala at the New York City Ballet as a guest of my friends Andrew and John; it was a long-planned outing that just a day ago had me filled with excitement. Now I was at the salon only because I had already paid for it.

The cognitive dissonance that hit me that night was so strong it felt almost gleeful, the way you feel when the ride on a roller coaster snaps your head back. The hem of my black satin skirt brushed the steps at Lincoln Center as I thought, *I don't have health insurance.* Andrew presented me with a champagne flute and I wondered, *What happens when I can't pay rent?* I was sitting only six rows from the stage where the dancers were moving through the intricate steps of choreography by Balanchine, mentally compiling an inventory of the food in my refrigerator. *Can a woman live on capers alone?*

I don't have an answer to that. Air America's board members and investors stepped in and anted up the money to save the newborn network. Al worked without a salary for a while, joking that he had become an involuntary investor. But the uncertainty of those days, when I didn't know if I would have a job or if we would be on the air, made me look more critically at why I had made the leap to Manhattan.

At the end of the gala that night, John was walking me to a cab. It is common at almost any fund-raising party or event in Manhattan for the attendees to get a gift bag as they exit, and this bash was no different. John handed me the glossy white bag and its contents — a book, a bottle of perfume, and other ephemera to represent the evening. As we walked out the door, a woman came up to us, her hair dyed red, her face slightly lined. It had gotten cold and she hunched her shoulders, pulled her collar close.

"Excuse me," she said, "are you keeping that gift bag? I collect them."

I looked at her. She had been waiting outside, in the cooling air, just to beg for a gift bag.

John hurried us along, but I found I couldn't stop thinking about her. I couldn't get the pathos of it out of my mind — what happens to people that they would do that, put import on something that shallow?

And then I wondered if I had done the same thing by moving to New York, if I had upset a good life close to friends and family, endangered a career, just so I could say I had gone to a bigger market, had worked on a national show — things that, in the end, weren't really so important.

I would like to tell you that I gave her my gift bag.

But I didn't.

I think it is fair to say that the majority of my colleagues at Air America wanted to do everything in their power to ensure that George W. Bush wouldn't get reelected.

I just wanted to cover the story.

If you considered my Air America colleagues as political evangelicals — burning with the spirit, filled with the mission — then I suppose I would have been an acolyte in the Church of the Mainstream Media. For all that the inhabitants of newsrooms are labeled "liberal" in their politics, my own experience has been that most of us adopt an attitude toward political parties that could best be described as "a pox on all their houses."

It's not that I don't believe in the political process. I do. I try to vote in every election, if only to honor the memory of the women who made it possible for me to cast a ballot, and because I believe that failure to exercise your franchise at the voting booth is a civic sin. An ambitious young newspaper colleague of mine in St. Paul made a very public declaration one fall that he was not going to vote because it was his professional duty to give every impression of impartiality; I was horrified and told him so at every opportunity. The idea isn't to disengage from society, it's to help make a better society through reporting the facts that help citizens make the most informed choices.

I believe in policies, not parties; in individuals, not platforms. I believe that power corrupts and that you often can trace the trail of wrongdoing by looking for the acquisition of power and money, not by simply checking the label "Republican" or "Democrat." Given the whispers I've heard from liberal staffers, I think there's just as much chance you'd find chauvinism among their think tanks and organizations as you would in conservative think tanks and organizations.

My coworkers at Air America wanted a specific result in the political process, and I was more interested in how we covered it. People like me have their place, but it isn't on political radio. So eventually I left. Despite the many kindnesses people showed me, I didn't belong there.

*   *   *

One of the ironies for me about being identified as a member of the liberal media is that, while I hosted a show on Minnesota Public Radio, I received constant criticism from a few sources on how I coddled conservatives. When you have been accused of being both too liberal and too conservative, you start to assume you are doing something right. At the very least, it makes you mistrustful of labels such as "liberal" and "conservative."

I should note, however, that public radio critics register their complaints in syntax that is practically Proustian compared to the profanity-littered e-mails, letters, and voice messages I used to receive at the newspaper and at KSTP. One critic of my column told me that he wanted to tie me up in a gunnysack and beat me with a stick; another sent me an entire screen of the rudest insults pertaining to my gender. Compare those messages to the missive I received just after I started on public radio: "Listening to Katherine Lanpher's attempts to master the technological details of her show is like being forced to watch an amateur chain-saw-juggling contest."

I miss those people. And I miss the electric anything-can-happen atmosphere of live radio. With Al, there were moments when I wanted to look through my fingers at him, the way you shield your eyes when you can't take the tension of a suspense film; I was never sure what would happen next. Like the time we decided to perform the entire show in the argot of pirates — Arrgh, me matey — and he challenged former Senator George McGovern, one of our guests, to a sword fight. Then there was the time he cast billionaire philanthropist George Soros as a goulash-serving waiter in a comedy skit.

One of my favorite moments happened early in my public radio career, when I first interviewed Albie Sachs, a South African freedom fighter who had been imprisoned during apartheid and who later lost the use of one eye and his right arm to a car bomb set by the South African security services. Now, he sits on the country's Supreme Court, sworn in by Nelson Mandela.

I had read about his days in solitary confinement, when he and another prisoner — a schoolteacher — ended up communicating with each other through song. Sachs would whistle to her, and the song of choice was Dvořák's "Going Home," a theme that the composer had picked up from a spiritual.

"What did it sound like?" I asked. "Could you do it for us?"

Justice Sachs closed his eyes, pursed his lips, and leaned into the microphone. When he was done, the notes seemed to hang in the air for a moment, fading away very slowly. And that's why I love radio. You get to whistle in the dark and everyone can hear it.

Iron and Clay

It is a december day in Paris and I am walking through the Luxembourg Gardens. The sky is overcast, the color of a shell, and in this light the buildings that surround the garden shimmer like gray pearls. There is no snow on the ground, just the flat, wide leaves left over from autumn, and they form a carpet of ivory and ocher and yellow around the Medici Fountain. The water from the fountain burls in the pool, and the marble lovers embrace; the topiary garlands and swags of ivy remain a vibrant green even in winter. The chairs that surround the pool are empty but still grouped in clusters, as if their inhabitants have only just left and will come back at any moment.

This is my first trip to Paris in more than six years, my first trip here since the divorce. I came with some odd notion of making Paris mine again, separate from my marriage and the trips to France that were part of that union. My husband and I came every year, and when we parted, I thought I was saying adieu to Paris as well; it seemed too painful to even think of coming back. But the woman who thought that way isn't around anymore. In her place is the woman who moved to New York and who, surviving that, now has the courage to reclaim her idealized city on her terms and no one else's.

I hadn't planned to start my first afternoon back in Paris with a trip to the Luxembourg Gardens, yet here I am, smiling at the memories that come back to me. I was a young wife here, eager and awkward in my attempts both to please my new French in-laws and to speak the language, and one Sunday afternoon in summer I came to this very fountain to seek a little respite. I can place that younger self on one of these chairs — her head tilted toward her book, her knees drawn up, the slack and casual carriage that sets apart and identifies most Americans here. I had the mien of a Midwestern woman, my face as open and guileless as a bread pan. It wasn't long before an older man came up to talk to me, heavyset, swarthy-faced, suspenders holding up his trousers. He was kind, asking me questions and complimenting my French — I'm sure I shone with pleasure — and then he asked me if I had seen the Statue of Liberty.

Most people know about the other replica of the statue that is in Paris, on a little island in the Seine near the Pont de Grenelle, but there is also one in the Luxembourg Gardens, a gift by the sculptor Auguste Bartholdi. My new *ami* took me by the arm to show me. Around us, children played in the sunshine, couples walked hand in hand, and the carousel animals went round in their circles. When we arrived at the statue, my new friend went to kiss me to show his affection for all *sympathique* Americans, and I complied at first — after all, this is how people greet each other here — but then his clutch turned distinctly less avuncular and I wrenched myself out of his embrace, backing away and then turning to flee, so ashamed at my credulity that my cheeks burned. In my memory, he laughed at my flight, and I wonder if I had turned back whether I would have found him settling into another chair, readying himself for the next little American mouse who might scuttle into the reach of his paws. When I walked into the dim, cool recesses of my mother-in-law's salon in her apartment on nearby Rue Saint-Placide, she and her sister and my husband were having tea. I sat down, trembling with relief.

"I shall always see Paris as the setting of a novel that will never be written," writes Julian Green, an American born in Paris who stayed on to live an exemplary life of letters. Despite his protestations, he went on to pen sixty-five books, including fiction. He might see Paris and see the setting of a novel that is not to be written; I see Paris and I see the possibility of transformation. I have this theory that we all have a city, an urban love that we take on as our own. I am living in New York, and I can feel the slow stitchery of affection taking hold, how I am becoming wedded to its streets and people.

But ask me which city I love, where my bones seem to ease and where I feel at home, and the answer isn't Manhattan. We all have a city, and mine is Paris.

I am one of its more hapless visitors. The first time I saw Paris, I was fleeced out of my cash within the first five minutes. I was a travel stripling, just a year or so into my career as a journalist. With all the insouciance of a woman in her early twenties, I had convinced myself that if I didn't travel to Europe right then, I might never make such a trip. Ever. So I blithely charged a two-week trip to London and Paris and embarked on my first solo journey abroad. My paternal grandmother — whose big trip in life had been to the 1962 world's fair in Seattle — had given me $100 and a security pouch for money that I could slip into my bra. Oh, how I laughed behind her back when I opened up that package.

The fates punish those who laugh at their grandmothers. I was a sleepy traveler when I arrived at the Gare du Nord in Paris, fumbling with my metro ticket, when a man offered to help me, pushing me through the turnstile with forceful hands. It wasn't until I tried to pay for a coffee at my hotel that I realized he had taken all of my money. I stumbled outside and was just about to take the subway back to the train station when I realized I didn't have the fare. It was Sunday; all the banks were closed. I had my passport and that was about it.

I started to snuffle, more at my own stupidity than anything else, when I heard a voice say, "Excuse me, are you American?" Thus began my first Parisian adventure as I was passed from helpmeet to helpmeet that day: the American expat who gave me his metro tickets, the French student and his Swiss girlfriend who helped me at the train station, the detective at the gendarme's desk who looked at me through wreaths of Gauloise smoke and smiled, asking in puzzlement because I didn't know the French word for "wallet," "Mademoiselle, you have lost your nurse?"

"No, no," I answered. "My purse."

Late in the day I happily discovered some franc notes tucked in a pocket of my jeans — just enough to buy a small bottle of wine, a disk of cheese, and a baguette. My room had a small balcony, and I opened the shutters to sit and look at the street life unfolding in front of me — the Art Nouveau curves of the wrought iron at the metro stop, the man in an apron and cap sweeping his portion of the sidewalk, the wares piled high in the windows of the different shops, the *boulangerie*, the *crémerie*, the *épicerie*. Even the names of the shops were beautiful to me, and I repeated them to myself as I sat on my little balcony. I had no idea how I would pay for the room or what would happen the next day, but I was so content. In that exact moment, I was exactly where I was supposed to be.

I feel that way again standing in the Luxembourg Gardens, and I am a little woozy on nostalgia as I pick my way down one of the wide, cream-colored pebbled paths that lead away from the Medici Fountain. I am strolling, my head lolled back to take in the sky, when I hear shouting. Ahead of me, three men in uniform are waving their arms. I wonder who they're shouting at and turn around to look. I can't see the object of their ire. I notice that the men are armed. Suddenly, it makes sense for me to stop moving, so I stand, my eyes darting over the landscape, trying to figure out what I should do next. Is it me they're after? *Moi?*

Oui.

As the uniformed men draw closer, I can see that two of them are scowling. It is the third man, tall and youthful, who approaches me and rattles off several sentences in French. I am translating far more slowly than he is speaking. It is as if I am a radio operator who can't quite get the frequency so that what I hear are words strung with lingual static: "Garden . . . evening . . . gates . . . whistles."

He peers at me and switches to English.

"Madame," he says, bending over to speak directly to the top of my head, "we are closed."

Comprehension dawns on my face.

"*Le jardin est fermé?*" I squeak in French, and my new escort grins in bemusement.

"*Oui.*"

I have a three-man escort to the tall, black wrought-iron gates of the Luxembourg Gardens, where the guards laugh and wave and wish me *bonne nuit* as they lock the door behind me.

If the city were a woman, I would be hooking a lock of her hair behind her ears, affectionately crooning, "Remember me? Remember me?" As it is, I am walking through the 5th and 6th *arrondissements* on pure muscle memory, my limbs knowing where to turn before I do. I stand on street corners and luxuriate in the sounds of the police and ambulance sirens, their Klaxon minuet that I had forgotten. I eavesdrop on conversations just to reacquaint myself with the wet slurry of sound that is French to me, the fullness in the mouth that it requires for an American to approximate the accent. An hour after being kicked out of the Luxembourg Gardens, just enough of my French returns that I can tell people who ask — and they do — what time it is, or nod in agreement when they complain about the car that whips around the corner too fast.

That the city comes wrapped in another language is part of its charm. I once sat across from an American woman at a gate at Charles de Gaulle Airport, part of a crush of people waiting for the same flight back to the States. She was heavyset and plain, dressed in dark, shapeless clothes. When she spoke English, she was unremarkable. When she spoke French, however, her whole face underwent a transformation; she became, if not beautiful, attractive. Her eyes lit up, the muscles of her face lifted, her lips seemed fuller as they rounded and extended to form the correct sounds and vowels. A Frenchman sitting next to her required help with his ticket, which is how I came to note her lingual makeover. He didn't know her, that was clear, so the glow she acquired came not from him but from who she became when she assumed the mantle of the French language. I believe that she became who she wanted to be: charming, assured, even chic.

I have an odd and ill-formed knowledge of Paris, hampered both by my romantic illusions and by the hodgepodge nature of my time here. It's true that, for more than a decade, I visited at least once a year; it's also true that I went for only a few days at a time. For my French family, my arrival in Paris was just a precursor to the real reason for the visit: our holiday in the country, where I would stay for a week before I returned to my American life and vacation schedule. (Every year, almost without fail, there would be a family discussion about the barbarity of my employer, who had given me so little vacation time, unlike the six weeks or so to which they were accustomed.) For years, whenever I read memoirs of Americans in Paris, I did so with a begrudging heart because the authors had been able to stretch their limbs, settle down, learn the language. I was there only long enough to provide evidence that, once again, I had failed to become fluent in French while living in Minnesota. It took the passage of time for me to realize that I had been given other gifts and that one of them was my mother-in-law.

She was the widow of a three-star general, and her proper title, as evidenced on the envelopes I saw cluttered on her mail tray, was *Madame la Générale.* She was a tiny woman with elegant cheekbones and white hair, and she was still beautiful when I knew her. A portrait from her youth, a black-and-white photograph from the 1930s, stood in its frame on a desk in the salon. Her head was cocked to one side, her mouth had a coquettish smile, and her hair was grooved in marcelled curls. It was still easy to see that face in the woman before me, aged some five decades.

Her husband had died a dozen years before I met her son, but I felt the presence of the general in the apartment, a place shadowed with dark wood and artifacts of the places they had lived during his years of service. There was an engraved bureau from Vietnam, a brass tray and leather chairs from Morocco. A pair of his old slippers peeked out from a corner in the *salle de bain,* and his coats still hung in one of the closets. Her son's room had not been altered since his student years, with peeling posters of theatricals on the walls, his collection of paperbacks still jammed on shelves, the same navy plaid coverlet on his twin bed. At night, V would sleep on a cot or on the floor and I would sleep on the narrow mattress he had used as a child. The air felt compressed with memories.

We usually arrived in late morning and were served a lunch that even now I can recall in its order and precision: perhaps a piece of terrine or a small crock of rillettes, the shreds of meat clinging to the fat on the knife; then a small chop, usually lamb, with haricots verts; then a salad with a simple vinaigrette; then a piece of fruit — a white peach, maybe, which V would peel for us; then small cheeses that were unwrapped, with tastes put on our plates; after that, a piece of tart perhaps; and then, finally, coffee. The meal would have been prepared by Conception, Madame's concierge from Portugal, a kind and efficient woman who raised two children, took care of Madame's needs, and also oversaw a fleet of other apartments, and whose husband, Tony, drove a taxi. Whenever I ran into her on the street, she would give me a broad smile and I would droop my head, if only because I felt so lacking in industry next to her bustling example.

If the meal was meant to revive us, it usually had the opposite effect on me. I would go from the false darts of energy that accompany me whenever I land after a long flight to a food-induced entropy and, after many excuses, would land on the navy plaid coverlet to sink into sleep. I would wake up to V gently shaking my shoulder and hissing in my ear that I shouldn't sleep so, that I wouldn't be able to fall asleep again that night. He was always right. I would sleepwalk through the next days of our visit, brightly waking up at three or four in the morning to turn on the little lamp next to the bed. Then I would read, sometimes putting down my book to study the shadows on the wall, to listen to the water running through the pipes, the fall of footsteps overhead — the quiet sounds of a Parisian apartment building at rest.

I was foreign there. When I was in high school, I made a forced march through the pages of Henry James's *The American,* groaning at the thought of even another chapter. What was the plight of Christopher Newman to me, a girl bored and itchy to leave the confines of this brick box of a high school? If he was so unhappy and ill-used, why didn't he just leave? When I visited Paris as a daughter-in-law, however, snatches of that text would come back to me, often when I was sitting in that dark bedroom, hemmed in by the books and artifacts of another life, another culture, another time. I felt like a piece of green, green wood dropped by mistake into an ornately carved and gilded Baroque chapel.

I was thick-limbed and thick-tongued, and even my appetites were outsize and clumsy. There wasn't a shop window I wasn't drawn to, a restaurant I didn't want to try, a food I didn't want to taste. I dawdled in front of a pastry shop window, pointing at the different treats. One looked particularly interesting, half coated in vanilla icing, half in chocolate. It was called *le divorce.*

"Katherine!" V said. "These are for children. You don't need any pastries!"

This is a detail I haven't thought about for years until I am walking again through the streets of the 6th *arrondissement.* I feel a jolt of recognition when I turn onto the Rue de Rennes, and then I find I am walking faster, sure of where I am, taking strides past the café where I would sit and have a Coca-Cola (for many years I was convinced they tasted better in Paris), noting with relief that the cheap clothing stores are still there, remembering a toy store that has disappeared. I am looking for something in particular and then I see it: a pair of green neon eyeglasses that hang at an angle over the window of an optometrist's shop, as if the building itself wanted to peer through them for a better look outside. This is the landmark for my mother-in-law's building, one that even I could approximate in my French, on each summer visit telling the cabdriver to look for *les lunettes vertes.* It is past dusk when I find the glasses, and they are glowing in the dark. I stand across the street and count up — the apartment is on the third floor, as the French count, fourth if you're American — until I see the windows, where the new occupants have pulled their white lace curtains shut tight.

I am so unself-consciously American that I once tried to tell my French mother-in-law about my marital troubles. I was in France on my own as a newspaper reporter, traveling through Paris after covering the fiftieth anniversary of D-day. I could conduct short interviews in French with people in the Normandy countryside, could pull memories from aged American veterans who didn't always want to return to cold times and dead comrades. But in the dining room on Saint-Placide, sitting across the table from *Madame la Générale,* I struggled, a hapless marital tourist trying to explain that I didn't get to see my husband enough, that he loved his theater more than me, that we needed more time together if our marriage were to survive.

Just to recall it makes me sigh; Christopher Newman would have fared better. And Henry James would have warned me against trying to convince a French mother that she should give up a little of her time with her only child, her son, who spent most of his year across the ocean for the sake of his theater.

Still, I had a moment where I thought she understood me. She was not unkind, *Madame la Générale.* Then there was a slight Gallic shrug of the shoulders, a little laugh, and the phrase *"Comme son père."* "Like his father." Then she looked at me and — I am guessing, because I don't know, will never know — willed me to understand what she had withstood, what she had tolerated and what I must too.

Only I chose not to, and after I divorced V in 1999, I never saw her again. She grew more frail, and Conception, whom she had long called *mon ange* — my angel — became a more constant presence in the apartment. In August 2003 I came home one day and pushed the button on the answering machine only to hear the hiss of long distance and a guttural voice that resembled V's, the words too garbled by grief to be clear. I didn't want the news to be true, so I phoned his different friends, hoping they would tell me that they had just talked to him, that everything was fine. No, no one had talked to him recently. All they knew was that he was in Paris for his annual holiday with his mother.

When I finally reached him, he confirmed that she was dead, one of the almost fifteen thousand victims of the vicious heat wave that swept through France that summer. Much has been made of the relatives who left their elderly to cope on their own, but V was a constant son. Her doctor had been blunt in his advice: she was dehydrating in the heat, but if V took her to the hospital, she might not get treatment in time; with the overcrowding, there was a danger she would die in a hallway. V kept his mother at home, he and Conception trying to get more fluids into her system, but when it was clear she was failing, her angels gathered around her and helped her leave this world. She was ninety-six.

"She was so beautiful at the end," he told me, his voice breaking, "so sweet."

I curled into a ball when I heard the news, slowly rocking with grief, the depth of which surprised me. The French for "mother-in-law" is *"la belle-mère,"* the beautiful mother. Yes, I know that I wasn't weeping for her alone. I was thinking of that afternoon when it was just the two of us, the dining room crowded with dark furniture, the old table covered with an oilcloth to preserve its finish, and of how we sat, staring at each other, unable to see what the other wanted, despite those green glowing glasses downstairs.

Now I stare at those glasses and use my rented cell phone to call V. "I'm in the neighborhood," I say. "I'm early."

I have such an attachment to these streets, to my history here, that what I want to say is "I'm home."

The voices of my women friends became positively feline when they heard that V was going to be in Paris at the same time I was. "Oh, *really?*" one of them said, stretching out the word. No, no, I protested, it's not like that. And, in truth, he wasn't on the itinerary when I planned the trip. I had called him to see if he knew a place I could stay; he had rented out his family's old apartment. When we discovered we were planning simultaneous trips to Paris and he proposed that we spend some time together, I was wary at first.

"This trip is about taking back my version of Paris," I told him. "I'm going to write about it, you know."

"Got it," he answered. "The theme is: poignant."

That made me laugh. I wait for him in front of La Grande Épicerie, the luxe Left Bank grocery. When I see him, my heart gives a little skip, despite it all. The years and the battles fall away and we walk, arm in arm, over to the Hôtel Lutetia for an aperitif, gossiping and catching up on family: How are his cousins Christine and Claude? How is Tante Miette? How is Conception?

I have rented a small apartment off the Rue Mouffetard in the 5th, and the landlords, new friends of mine in New York, tell me that George Orwell lived just a few doors down when he was a young man. The street is called the Rue du Pot de Fer — the iron pot — and V smiles when he hears the name. "There is an old fable," he tells me, "with the iron pot and the clay pot." I look it up later myself — it is from La Fontaine. An iron pot asks a pot of clay to go on a journey. The clay pot is fearful and wants to stick by the hearth, convinced he'll get shattered on the bumpy road. No, no, soothes the iron pot. "If something hard in view / By chance endangers you / Between you two I'll go / And save you from the blow." Thus convinced, the clay pot sets off with the iron pot, but the journey ends very soon, for the clay pot is smashed into shards, just as he predicted.

V walks me to the apartment, and we trek up five flights of spiral staircase and settle down in the small salon, at the table by the windows that have a view of the courtyard below and the dome of the Panthéon. And what we do next is — well, I guess it was to be expected, two people who still love each other, in Paris, looking out at the moon.

We play cards. Gin rummy, to be exact, the game we played when we got engaged, the game we played so many nights of our marriage, the game we gave up when we divorced. We don't even talk that much about it, really. We start looking for the cards in the apartment, and when we don't find them, we go to the small stores on Rue Mouffetard and buy a deck. Our memory of the rules — How many points do you need before you can put down your cards? How many cards do you deal? — is hazy at first but gets stronger with each game. While we play, we talk — about our marriage, our divorce, our history. We cry about the child we wanted and couldn't have, about decisions made, about time gone by. We laugh about the silliness of the game, the ardor of our competition (we both hate to lose), the pleasure that can be derived from hearts and spades and diamonds and clubs. We play cards every night that I am in Paris.

"This is not what I came here for," I protest, and he laughs and deals again.

We fall into other old patterns. I still annoy him with my habit of stopping to inspect the windows of every other shop, so he is nearly a block ahead of me, in midsentence, before he turns around to find that I am dumbstruck by a pair of smart leather gloves with little bows at the wrist. Another time, it is the display of a Nativity crèche in the window of a *fruiterie*, with dried fruits that glisten like jewels. I am like one of those small dogs who must stop and sniff at every doorway to gather the canine news, with halts and starts and long pauses.

I don't spend all my time with my ex-husband. I am by myself the day I discover the hat lady on the Rue Dauphine, a small shop with chapeaus piled on old vanities, on chairs, on black shelves that go from ceiling to floor. Two elderly women stand in the center of the shop, one with a cane, the other with a bandage wrapped around her ankle for support. They have white hair and pale faces and could be sisters; they remind me, in fact, of Madame and her sister. As I browse, I take pleasure in listening to the fluted tones of their voices. They chirp and coo like two gray doves over this grave dilemma, the purchase of a hat for the winter.

"But does it go with the fur?"

"Is it warm enough?"

"No, no, it is not smart. Try this."

The milliner stalks the store, pulling out hats for all of us to try, thrusting a bowl of chocolates in our faces, occasionally pulling on her glasses to dispense sartorial advice. At one point, she leans over to me and, in a confidential tone, says in English, "If you can wait while I help these two, then I can show you some really magnificent hats."

The sisters, however, are not to be rushed. "Oh, *c'est mignon*," one of them says when I try on a maroon-and-beige knitted tam. These women have all day, the milliner does not, so soon enough she is showing me what she calls "her babies," fantastical creations of linen and organza and tissue-thin horsehair called *crin*. The tam is replaced with an unearthly concoction of gradually rising disks of sheer vanilla and caramel-colored *crin* that sits at an angle on my head. I feel like a large, elegant bird, as if I should walk by lifting each ringed avian foot with purpose.

The milliner looks at me thoughtfully.

"Hats have a lot to do with psychology," she says.

I raise my eyebrows.

"It starts at the head and there it stays," she continues, warming to her subject. *"Oui, oui,* it is the beginning of psychology. You look in the mirror and you see yourself. Let's say a woman comes in and she is not very pretty, she is not very young, she is not very rich. I help her find the right hat and then she looks in the mirror and she likes what she sees."

I buy two hats.

I don't know if I am the woman she is referring to who is not very pretty, not very young, and not very rich, but I have had days when I have fit all those categories. But when I am walking down the street in one of my new hats, I feel as if I have gained some semblance of my own sense of Paris. And what is it? Nothing much, really — to look in the mirror and be content with what I see and then to join the others on the street, all of us made of iron and of clay.

On Location

THEY ARE FILMING A MOVIE in my neighborhood. One day you come home and the parked cars that usually line both sides of the street have disappeared, leaving the thoroughfare looking as plucked as a bare-limbed tree in winter. A couple of hulking white trailers move in, with papered-over windows, and generators that fill the air with a low and ceaseless hum. A regiment of self-important-looking people stalk the sidewalks, using walkie-talkies or headset phones to communicate with people you suspect are just across the street. You simply want to get to the hardware store, but as the crew members look at you with a cool air of dismissal, you realize that, at least for now, they own these streets and you are the interloper.

To live in New York means that on any given day you can

stumble upon a movie set or the taping for a popular television series or a photo shoot for a magazine. The first time, you feel a frisson of excitement, to think that you are living this close to the stories and the pictures and the images that will go out to a nation, a world. And, of course, you crane your neck to see if there are any recognizable faces, any names that you can drop in conversations with people back home. Then it becomes, well, pedestrian. A friend and I were walking down Perry Street one night when a man we didn't know came running up to us, breathless and bug-eyed. "Quick!" he said in a stage whisper. "Quick! Right ahead, if you hurry you can still see them. It's Matthew Broderick and his wife!" We laughed and maintained our leisurely pace, amused that Broderick's starstruck fan didn't identify the couple the way most of the country would have — as Sarah Jessica Parker and her husband. "He's obviously a theater person," my friend said dryly.

A few months after I moved here, I walked out of my apartment and into a maze of yellow police tape. I was talking on my cell phone and didn't take much notice at first. "They're taping an episode of *Law and Order*," I said with some amusement.

Then I turned a corner and saw the stricken faces of the bystanders. These weren't people hoping for a glimpse of Sam Waterston; these were the neighbors of the man whose body had just come out on a gurney.

"What happened?" I asked, and someone pointed to the

building, told me that a resident had been killed. "Murder," the person said.

There are always two kinds of stories going on in New York, the real and the unreal. Sometimes it's hard to assess which is which.

The movie crew on my block is filming at night, and the bright lights they use give an unearthly cast to the sky outside my windows, as if there were a full moon at street level. In the first months after my cross-country migration, I would track the progress of the moon's path across the sky from my tiny terrace. The abundance of ambient light in the city means that most of the landmarks of the evening sky disappear; the moon became one of the few familiar celestial sights that had traveled with me. Sometimes I would call a friend in St. Paul and he would look out from his window at the moon over the Mississippi and tell me what he saw, just to make sure we were both looking at the same extraterrestrial body.

I am nearing the two-year anniversary of my arrival in New York. When people I meet ask how long I've been in the city, sometimes they also ask if the move was worth it.

I don't know.

Whenever I'm homesick for my old life, people here say, "Well, you can always go back." I suppose that is true. I still own a house there and have friends so close I could count them as family. But the person I used to be, the life I used to lead — those are gone, irrevocably altered by the leaps of the past two years. If I went back to Minnesota, some part of me would look at the moon there, set against all the stars, and wonder if it looked the same against the Manhattan skyline. I'd have to call someone just to check.

When I go back to St. Paul, I usually stay with Helena and Michael, friends who live directly across the street from my house. When I still lived on that avenue, I used to walk into their home nearly every day. We rarely locked our doors, and, at night, if I wanted company, I would light a small candle I had placed by the front door, just inside my porch. We called it the "beacon," and its glow signaled that I was open to receiving visitors. Not that long ago, Michael was in Manhattan on business and came over to my place in the Village for dinner. We were reminiscing and catching up on neighborhood gossip when he spied a framed black-and-white photograph of my old front porch in St. Paul. He crossed the room and picked it up.

"You know," he said, "I always thought this would be forever."

We had lived in a momentary universe of such ease and friendship, days and seasons marked by the most pleasurable and pedestrian of pursuits. We held a block party each summer, parking cars at either end of the street to barricade our avenue so we could play games of foursquare and so the younger kids could ride their bikes with abandon, weaving fearlessly from curb to curb. One year, the adults joined the kids in a game of kick-the-can, and I ran until I got a stitch in my side. On the first day of school, we would corral the kids and pose them on someone's front steps for pictures. You knew Halloween was approaching when the pumpkin stand opened up for business in the church parking lot nearby; if the weather was fine enough, we would gather in somebody's front yard and carve our jack-o'-lanterns as a group. One winter, Michael and Helena flooded their backyard, turning it into a skating rink. I could stand on my porch, looking into the inky night, and listen to the rasp of blades on ice, to the sweet sounds of kids whooping and hollering as they chased one another on their skates.

The first time I came back from New York to revisit my old life, my house was empty, and as I walked through the rooms, my steps echoed against the walls. I went up into the attic and peered through a little window at my favorite view: that of the rooftops of my old neighborhood stretching on for blocks. The fact that I had left all this hit me hard. I knew then that, even if I came back, it would never be the same. What had I done? I knelt on a packing box and wept.

Last December I was staying with Michael and Helena, and at one point I wrapped myself in a shawl and stepped outside onto their porch. A streetlight cast shadows on the little hill of my old front yard, where so many neighborhood kids had played. I looked at the house — the broad porch, the green roof, the cream-colored stucco — with affection, but I also thought that maybe it was time to move on, that maybe I needed to admit that the house and my dreams could part company. Had anyone walked by, they would have thought I was whispering to myself, but I was talking to the house, to the woman who used to live there.

"I can let you go," I said, "It's OK. It's time to let go."

Where does that leave me? I'm not sure. I am slowly building a life here in New York, gathering friends and connections. A friend who used to live here in the 1980s warned me before I moved to Manhattan that the city can sharply reflect one's moods and fortune. "When you're having a good day, the city sparkles," he told me. "When you're having a bad day, the city is ugly."

I've had bad days. Once, I had to hail a cab outside my office, dragging two pieces of luggage in a driving rain. I needed to go back to my apartment to retrieve some things I had forgotten for a cross-country trip. I was in a hurry and didn't want to miss my plane. The cabdriver was hostile from the moment he pulled up. I don't know if it was my dripping luggage or my face, but he yelled at me when I asked him to turn around and take me downtown, and he yelled at me when I tried to pay him with a twenty-dollar bill, and we yelled at each other when he insisted he couldn't give me change. He pulled up to my building and aligned the car in front of a large puddle, the doors and trunk snapping open as if the car were pursing its lips and spitting me out into the wet: *Puh-tooey!* The wind blew my umbrella inside out. By the time the cab pulled away, I was wet and angry and bedraggled, and tears were arcing from my eyes as if I were a cartoon character.

One of my neighbors was standing in front of my building, and she came over with an umbrella.

"Are you all right?" she asked in a thick New York accent.

I was practically hiccuping in anger.

"Have you ever (hiccup), ever (hiccup), had a bad (hiccup) New York day?" I asked.

"Ohhhhhhhhhhhhhh," she said, going through about five tone changes. "Yeah. I have. I know exactly what you mean."

I have good days too: My friend Julie is celebrating her fiftieth birthday, and her girlfriend Laura arranges for a nighttime helicopter ride over Manhattan; I eagerly accept the invitation to join them. While we wait our turn at the helipad office on a narrow hurricane-fenced strip alongside the Hudson, Julie makes so many nervous jokes that, despite the fact it is her birthday, I ban two words from her vocabulary: "crash" and "sink."

But when we are up in the air, different words occur to us. In the helicopter, suspended in the sky, we look down on a city riveted with jewels. The headlights from the traffic heading downtown merge into a stream of flowing, molten gold. The taillights of the traffic headed uptown glitter like rubies. We head north along the west side of Central Park, stunning not only for the trees threaded with light but also for the dark spaces — such as the reservoir — which register as velvet pauses against all the brightness.

We circle the Statue of Liberty and get so close that we can see into the naked light that illuminates her crown; looking at it without any shielding surface is a little like looking directly into the sun.

It's Julie who notes that the lights in all the buildings look like diamonds from one direction but pearls from another. And it's Julie who tells me later that if I ever get lost on the island, I should look for the Empire State Building.

"Think of it," she says, "as your North Star."

Sailors use the North Star to help them navigate, to get home, but I am still trying to figure out where my home is. I don't know. It's a feeling that reminds me of that trapeze lesson, that moment when you have to make the decision to jump or not, to leap or stay on the platform.

When I first moved to Manhattan, I fell in love with riding the subway. Each morning when I walked to my station at Christopher Street, I might as well have been a character in a movie, my own routine actions so new that they felt unreal. Here is a woman walking to the subway, I told myself, here is a woman who lives in New York. I studied the people around me on the subway cars as if they were characters too: a young Latina mother holding her squirmy kid, a pride of fresh-faced police recruits chatting in their academy uniforms, a black youth wearing a jacket with Al Pacino as Scarface painted on the back, a trio of Pakistani girls bickering about their homework. You could see everyone, it seemed, at some point on the subway line, and I marveled at the fact that people brought books to read, buried their faces in paperbacks and textbooks and newspapers. Who would want to miss a moment of this ever-changing spectacle?

Now it's two years later, and I am a woman who lives in New York and who is riding the subway. I am traveling from the Upper East Side back to Greenwich Village. I am going home. I have my book; on this day it is a new memoir by Haven Kimmel, so that even while I am sitting underneath the city of Manhattan, part of me is in Kimmel's hometown of Mooreland, Indiana. I am able to read while I wait for the local and then again while I wait to switch to the express line. I keep my place in my book with my thumb when I hop from one car to the next, and I read while I stand in a shuddering car, leaning against a metal railing for support. I tuck the book under my arm while I walk through the white-tiled walls beneath Grand Central to the shuttle that will take me across to Times Square. There, I stride briskly through the crowds of commuters barreling to their next train wearing overcoats and carrying briefcases, tourists standing in confused clusters and consulting their maps. A young Asian man with purple-tipped hair is playing an electric guitar, a rug spread out in front of him to catch the bills and change that people throw as they pass by. I wait for the No. 2 Express down Seventh Avenue to the Village, and when the car pulls into the 14th Street station, I walk out and take my position next to a set of dingy gray stairs that leads up to 13th Street. The local train arrives and I get on. When it finally pulls into my stop at Christopher, I walk directly out of the subway car and into the turnstile. I push with my body and my book, and the metal arms allow me to pass, and finally I pause, looking at the four staircases before me that could take me up and out into a city with so many corners and so many stories, both real and unreal. I choose a set of stairs. I go up.

Acknowledgments

Thanks go first to the women of Springboard Press — both past and present — who helped me make the leap to print: former publisher Jill Cohen and especially editorial director Karen Murgolo, who showed me such kindness during the writing process. Thanks as well to Matthew Ballast, Jason Bartholomew, Karen Landry, and Jessica Kaufman.

This book wouldn't be in your hands at all without the faith and tenacity of literary agent Marly Rusoff, who really is a marvel. I am fortunate to know John Habich, not only because he is such a good friend but also because of his keen editorial eye. He sharpened the manuscript considerably.

Shannon Olson and Deborah Keenan are two writers I'm proud to know and even luckier to count as friends; they gave me day-to-day and sometimes hour-to-hour support when it was sorely needed. The elegant Patricia Hampl sent me words of wise counsel, and Helena Pohlandt-McCormick is a gentlewoman and a scholar, not to mention a grand neighbor.

Joanna Coles first led me to *More* magazine, where editor in chief Peggy Northrop made me feel welcome. I'm grateful to them, especially for assigning me to work with Liz Ozaist, a dream of an editor. Michael Newman is no longer on the op-ed page of the *New York Times,* but he opened a door there for me: thank you.

Every writer needs an audience, and I had the Memphis Book Club, culled from my neighbors upstairs in New York, who were happy to hear the latest draft: Julie Gold, Laura Pearson, John Byrne, and Joe Saccoccio.

Two former colleagues at the *St. Paul Pioneer Press* also lent assistance: Martha Malan and Chuck Laszewski, as did a new colleague here in New York: Lauren Cerand.

Early readers of portions of these pages include Jacqui Banaszynski, Mary Kay Blakely, Fawn Bernhardt, Judy Brunswick, Francesa DiJosia, Kathleen Fluegel, Lainey Giffen, Wendy Goodman, Felicity Jones, Elizabeth Merrick, Theresa Monsour, Kate Parry, John Schneeman, Jessica Seigel, and Kristin Tillotson.

Elaine C. Weiss is a dear friend and I love her to pieces. Craig Duff shoehorned me out of my apartment when I needed to go out, and I would expire if John Schneeman didn't live near me in the Village.

Al Franken brought me to New York, and Franni Franken made sure I survived my induction. I thank them both with affection.

Acknowledgments

I thank Vincent Gracieux for our years together and for his understanding.

I thank Steven Phillip Woodward for his love and affection, and for the sculpture that rests in my Manhattan aerie.

The stories in this book are the stories of my life as I remember them; I have changed some names of my childhood friends to ensure their privacy.

When I was a little girl, my father took me downstairs to his workshop and gave me my own hammer and taught me how to pound in a nail. My mother, meanwhile, read to me at lunch, acting out parts from the classics. (Note: She does a fine Mr. Toad from *The Wind in the Willows*.)

In other words, my parents taught me tenacity and a love for books. I can't think of a better preparation for the writing life. Whatever good resides in these pages — it's for them.

About the Author

Katherine Lanpher's writing has appeared in *More* magazine and the *New York Times*. The former host of Minnesota Public Radio's *Midmorning* show, she was also a columnist for the *St. Paul Pioneer Press*. She moved to Manhattan on Leap Day 2004 to join *The Al Franken Show* on Air America Radio, where she stayed until last fall. She still lives in New York City.